WHEN LOST MEN COME HOME

Endorsements

David Zailer goes beyond recovery to keys to revitalize your spiritual vitality. This book is a great plan to get your life back if it has been stolen by the cheap thrills of sexual and moral compromise.

Stephen Arterburn
Author & Founder of Women of Faith & Host of NewLife "Live"
www.newlife.com

I find David Zailer's book, *When Lost Men Come Home*, to be a very personally and scripturally sound approach to the wisdom of the Twelve Steps. It is very powerful indeed — and a much needed alternative to the purely secular books on working the Steps. Only through the power of personal transparency, as provided in these pages, will sex addiction come "Out of the Shadows" of ignorance and shame that has bound it for so very long. My prayers continue to be with David and his powerful ministry.

Dr. Mark Laaser
Faithful and True Ministries
www.faithfulandtrueministries.org

When Lost Men Come Home by David Zailer provides a transparently honest narrative of the hopelessness of addiction and the hopefulness of recovery through Christ. I am convinced the Lord will use *Lost Men* to bring hope and direction to those who are still lost in their addiction.

Reverend Laird Bridgman, Psy.D, C.E.A.P.
www.rsaministries.org

Dave Zailer is no stranger to struggle or honesty. In *When Lost Men Come Home,* he speaks light into a tender area of our lives that prefers to remain in darkness. "At some point in their lives, most men (and women too) will struggle with sexual integrity." This needed book not only helps us understand the progressive nature of sexual addiction, but provides a specific process and way out of the pain that consumes so many people's lives.

Joey O'Connor
Author & Executive Director, The Grove Center for the Arts and Media
www.thegrovecenter.org

While I've personally counseled thousands of men in their own recovery journeys, it is the wisdom, grace and love from God, as revealed in this book you're holding, which has touched those men's lives through me, and for that I will always be grateful. You can thank God you found *When Lost Men Come Home*!

Jayson Graves, M.MFT
Founder & Clinical Director for Healing for the Soul
www.healingforthesoul.org

For those that have suffered with this sensitive subject, *When Lost Men Come Home* reads like a tall drink of cool water. David Zailer's authentic truth-telling of how he survived to tell his story of struggle and turning to faith give the reader hope without feeling judged. Having counseled many women whose lives have been disappointedly disrupted due to unfaithfulness of the mind and spirit, I know this book will be the encouragement that is needed to restore relationships and to give untold numbers the opportunity to truly live the life they so desire to live.

Leesa Bellesi
The Kingdom Assignment Foundation, Author and Speaker
www.kingdomassignment.org

At our treatment center, we attempt to reach the whole man and his underlying issues that keep him trapped in his addictions to drugs and alcohol. Most of our male clients come to us with early-childhood sexual abuse issues or sexual addiction as a co-occurring disorder. We have found Dave's book to be insightful, practical and effective, and we have adopted it as a valued component of our curriculum. *When Lost Men Come Home* gives men the hope that helps transform their compulsions into sobriety and their brokenness into lives of integrity.

Richard E. Jackson, CEO
Pacific Hills Treatment Centers, Inc.
www.pachills.com

This book, When Lost Men Come Home, will be particularly helpful for men and women who are interested in combining the venerable Twelve Step concepts with the Word of God. That's a powerful combination!

Dr. Ron Shackelford
MFT, CSAT (Certified Sex Addiction Therapist)
www.SexHelp4Porn.com

As a Christian pastor who struggled with sex addiction, I am so thankful for Operation Integrity and *When Lost Men Come Home*. God has used this book along with one-on-one counseling to transform me into what He wanted me to become. Previously, I had been critical of Twelve Step programs, but this book has helped me to better see I needed help and the various ways God would bring me the help I needed. My wife and I still use *When Lost Men Come Home* for everyday devotional reading and to supplement our growth as believers.

James
Pastor in West Virginia

When I first read David Zailer's *When Lost Men Come Home,* it was so compelling I could not put it down. So I know it will touch you deeply, leaving you inspired. David has a quality that few people have... brutal honesty! It is refreshing to have someone write so transparently, with the simple purpose of helping others heal.

Jerry Sinclair
Faithful & True Ministries of Jacksonville, Florida Inc. (501c3)
www.southpointbaptist.org/psalm51.htm

Operation Integrity and *When Lost Men Come Home* saved me from crashing and hitting the bottom by diverting my downward spiral path into an upwards godly path. And this happened even before I fully realized I was headed straight for destruction. The way God uses David Zailer and *When Lost Men Come Home* as a tool to change lives is a wondrous miracle in itself. I will forever thank God for what He has done for me and my family through David, this book, and *Operation Integrity*.

Chris
Fireman from California

I believe David Zailer's book, *When Lost Men Come Home*, is the finest resource available for those seeking a Christ-centered Twelve Step recovery program for sex addiction. David shares parts of his own story in an engaging way that is helpful to both individuals and groups who want to recover from this devastating condition. This book draws you in, making you feel like you are part of an Operation Integrity meeting, being encouraged by those recovering through this program. More than anything, this book gives hope. It is a wonderful resource, both for those in recovery and for those who accompany them.

Mark
Pilot from Tennessee

When I met David Zailer, I realized quickly that we shared much philosophical common ground at the clinical and spiritual levels. In our work as a recovery ministry, faith community, and treatment center, many of our clients have backstories that include sexual abuse and addiction, so it is comforting to know that David and Operation Integrity are there to help in these areas. Our clients have told us how much *When Lost Men Come Home* has helped them, and as one client in particular said, "finally a book about my issues that I can really understand."

Dave Brisbin, MDiv, RASI
Lead Pastor, theeffect
www.theeffect.org

When Lost Men Come Home is a practical approach to recovery through the Twelve Steps. David Zailer uses his own poignant journey to guide readers through a process that he aptly describes as both simple and hard. Those struggling with sex addiction will find help through David's guidance.

Milton S. Magness, D Min, MA Psy, CSAT,
Author of *Hope & Freedom for Sexual Addicts and Their Partners* and *Thirty Days to Hope & Freedom from Sexual Addiction*
www.hopeandfreedom.com

When Lost Men Come Home tackles one of the most prevalent and hidden issues of our day and David Zailer is just the guy to do it. Cutting quickly to the core, Dave knows the only hope to free people from their addictions is spiritual growth. Filled with clear ideas and powerful first-person experience, this book is a great resource for anyone struggling with sexual integrity.

Todd Gorton
Coast Hills Church – Pastor, Communication & Worship Arts
www.coasthillschurch.org

David Zailer's book, When Lost Men Come Home, not only personifies issues related to successful addiction recovery but also communicates principles important to everyone desiring an authentic walk with Christ.

Pastors Sheryl and Todd from Ohio

When Lost Men Come Home is an inspiring read and study for anyone who wants to restore their sanity from the ravages of sexual addiction, and for those who want to make right their relationship with God – some for the first time. Through revealing personal glimpses into the author's own journey, David Zailer invites the reader to surrender their addiction for a life of integrity. Never heavy-handed, those who have spent time on their own spiritual quest will want to walk along beside him and re-examine their own definition of a Higher Power. This book is a must read for men and women who want to "come home" in their own spiritual quest and how it relates to their recovery from sexual addiction.

Alexandra Katehakis, Founder and Clinical Director
Center for Healthy Sex, Los Angeles, CA
http://www.thecenterforhealthysex.com/

This book, *When Lost Men Come Home,* speaks clearly into a difficult and frightening reality of human experience. David Zailer has a way of blending scriptural principles with the time proven effectiveness of the Twelve Step recovery movement. He speaks from his own inspired journey, revealing important factual truth, and boldly sharing God's promise to transform lives. Read this book and then share it with someone else. It may save your life and someone else's too.

Terry LaDow MS
BCPCC, CADC II
www.terryladow.com

I have had the privilege of working with men with addictions for the past 10 years. David Zailer's book *When Lost Men Come Home* has been the "go-to" book I recommend for sexual addiction. His warm, caring manner and his honest, humble heart towards those who struggle with sexual addiction create an environment for healing that emanates from deep within, where the struggle takes place. David uses the simplicity of the Twelve Steps along with his deeply personal relationship with Christ to lead lost men to a fulfilling life of peace, freedom and joy.

Nina Dreyer, LCSW
Clinical Director of Encompass Recovery
www.theeffect.org

I consider David Zailer to be a co-warrior with me on the front lines of spiritual warfare. We have fought together in several battles to stand in the gap for Christ in a hyper-sexualized world which attacks Christians and families on many fronts. David's book is honest, real, and powerful in making the point that one will find victory only from a deep and abiding relationship with Christ. Read *When Lost Men Come Home;* and be armed for battle.

Rev. Bill Berry
Founder & Director of Battle Plan Ministry
www.battleplanministries.org

WHEN LOST MEN COME HOME

A Journey to Sexual Integrity

by

David Zailer

Published by Homecoming Books for Operation Integrity

ISBN 10 0615598239
13 978-0-615-59823-9

Printed in the United States of America
Cover Art by 3 AM Communication
Cover Photo by Betty Pauline Haines
Special thanks to Patty Kennedy for editorial assistance

Acknowledgements

Thanks and appreciation to…

Those who currently serve or have served on the Board of Directors for Operation Integrity. They prove God's redeeming love is real.

The men who participate in the Operation Integrity fellowship that meets on Monday nights at Coast Hills Community Church. Their wisdom speaks throughout these pages.

The professionals who help develop literature and programs in Operation Integrity.

The people and staff of Coast Hills Community Church, a real life community of faith and vision.

A double dose of appreciation to Patty Kennedy of Springfield, Missouri, who lives her life lovingly as a wife, mother and grandmother, all while superhumanly conquering bad grammar and run-on sentences.

For those who know they need help.

TABLE OF CONTENTS

INTRODUCTION

Several years before I wrote the first edition of this book, I started writing about my own experience recovering from sexual addiction. I don't recall exactly what motivated me to put my thoughts on paper. The only thing I can remember was the hope that somehow, someway the experiences shared between me and others could be helpful to someone in the future.

I lived alone at the time and after work each day I came home and sat hour after hour, hunting and pecking on my computer keyboard, producing piles of incoherent, unintelligible mish-mash — kind of like this sentence. I never thought of it as personal, but it was. I never thought of my writing as important, but looking back now, I can see how it has become very important to me and to others. A few months into this process, I was asked by someone at church to facilitate a sexual addiction recovery group for men in our local community. I wasn't thrilled with the idea, but my friend and others pointed out there was no one better equipped than me to do it. (Very few people have excelled in obsessive lustfulness like I have.) Our group started small at first with a grand total of three men. Then we had 4, then 6, 10, 15, 20, and it continued to grow. The men came from all walks of life, each with a strong desire to change their lives.

Today, our group consists of a construction worker, a medical doctor, a marketing analyst, a computer programmer, a rocket scientist (yes, a rocket scientist), a software engineer, a university professor, an eye doctor, a dentist, a welding supervisor, an airline pilot, a real estate developer, a home builder, a musician, several businessmen, a retired football coach, a salesman, a school teacher, two engineers, a couple members of the clergy, a political consultant and a contractor. We are a mixed bag of nuts, and — for the most part — a very merry band of characters.

As more and more men came to our group, I continued to write, but my writing took a new direction. With these men, I became more of a listener and observer, so I began writing more about what I heard from them than what I knew to write on my own. I facilitated less and less, finding more interest in what these men had to say than what my own experience provided. I sensed that each of these men had an important voice to share. Sitting at the keyboard in the evenings, I was no longer simply writing; I was working to capture the thoughts and feelings of these men, which helped me to capture my own thoughts and feelings.

We are convinced that most people will struggle with their sexual integrity — or lack thereof — at some time in their life. Many men and women have re-recurring problems with their sexual behavior and, increasingly, there is an awareness that people can and often do become addicted to sex in one way or another. The impact on lives and marriages is staggering, crossing all social, ethnic and religious boundaries. The great tragedy is that most people don't know, won't accept and can't admit that they have a struggle, a problem or an addiction and even if they did recognize it, where would they go?

Every man in our group knows the struggle, which when ignored turned into a problem, and when left unrecognized progressed into addiction. Thankfully we got help and recognized that we were addicted. We freely admit our struggles, problems and addictions and, having done so, we have begun to recover from them.

It is our belief that most people do want to lead lives of sexual integrity. We have seen the carnage all around us, having caused more than a little of our own. We know what our decisions have cost us and others in terms of our relationships, our marriages, our children, time, money and energy. And thankfully, we have seen that there is a way to change our lives.

Through a Christ-centered application of a Twelve Step recovery process, we are experiencing a transforming movement back toward sexual health. Each of us is discovering an enthusiastic expectation of a healthy life and developing our own personal voice with which we can confidently share a message of gracious encouragement and accountability with one another.

The following pages are the heard, observed and expressed experience of our shared group life, as well as certain parts of my personal recovery journey. No one stands above anyone else. Together, our individual solos have grown into a collective chorus. We speak together as one body, united in voice, inviting and challenging you to be free as we are becoming free. We are the sound of men, struggling mighty men, sharing our lives personally, deeply, in forthright honest and transparent unison. We don't own the song of freedom we sing. The song of freedom belongs to God. He sang it to us and we sing it to you. We invite you to discover the freedom your heart longs to know.

Find your voice and sing along.

David Zailer

THE PROBLEM

Addiction is a medical and clinical term referring to physiological and psychological dependencies that exhibit themselves in destructive behavioral patterns. In layman's terms, *addiction is a destructive relationship with any mood or mind altering substance or experience.* It is a complex human phenomenon that is manifested in physical, psychological, sociological and spiritual ways. It has been called the most human of all diseases or conditions, and *no one is immune.*

Sexual addiction is one of the most misunderstood of all addictions. Simply stated, *sexual addiction is the loss of control over destructive sexual behavior or relationship.* Perhaps the most helpful definition is a practical one: sexual behavior that has a negative effect on one's life. A "sex addict" is someone who utilizes their sexual experience(s) to alter their mood or state of mind in a way that is destructive to them and their relationships. Most often thought of as inappropriate sexual behavior, sexual addiction can also be present in those who have no apparent inappropriate behavior. Even married monogamous people can be addicted sexually if they depend on "appropriate" sex to maintain their sense of well-being. Sexuality is an essential part of human life. But, when a person uses sexuality as if it were a drug to medicate their mood, the healthy spectrum of the sexual experience is eroded and it becomes destructive, and addictive. In fact, sexual addiction is not really about sex at all, it is about intimacy. Sexual addiction is a common result when sexuality is substituted for healthy intimacy.

To be alive is to be addicted, and to be alive
and addicted is to stand in need of grace.
Gerald G. May MD, *Addiction & Grace*

A SOLUTION

The vision of Operation Integrity is to help people recover from addiction, leading to radical life transformation. We accomplish this by educating people about addiction, helping people become part of a community that supports recovery and growth, encouraging spiritual growth through a personal Twelve Step program along with counseling and/or therapy, and Spiritual Formation leading to an ever-deepening relationship with God. We propose that the following five components be part of a person's life — minimum of three to five years.

- Meet personally with a qualified therapist or counselor as often as possible and as guided by the counselor. Involve one's family in therapy as suggested by counselor.
- Be involved in a Christ-centered Twelve Step Recovery Group. This includes attending meetings like Operation Integrity and other addiction specific support fellowships.
- Be involved in Twelve Step process at a personal level. This includes getting a sponsor and following their guidance, thoughtfully and devotionally reading recovery material like *When Lost Men Come Home* and other related literature.
- Encourage family involvement through Counseling, Al-Anon, Co-Dependents Anonymous, or similar Twelve Step support fellowship for spouses and loved ones.
- Address underlying triggers. Underlying causes may be an excessive need for affirmation, family of origin issues, childhood abuse or abandonment, unhealed grief, deep feelings of inferiority or superiority, an unhealthy view of God which may even exist in those who have religious training and church experience. Other causes may include other addictions like overeating, alcohol and other drugs, gambling, unhealthy relationships, religious activity and others.

It has been the Operation Integrity experience, that people who follow these suggestions with diligence and sincerity have a successful recovery experience.

THE TWELVE STEPS

Step One We admitted we were powerless over our addictions, that our lives had become unmanageable.

Step Two We came to believe that a Power greater than ourselves could restore us to sanity.

Step Three We made a decision to turn our will and our lives over to the care of God as we understood Him.

Step Four We made a searching and fearless moral inventory of ourselves.

Step Five Admitted to God, to ourselves, and to another human being the exact nature of our lives.

Step Six We became entirely ready to have God remove all these defects of character.

Step Seven We humbly asked Him to remove our shortcomings.

Step Eight We made a list of all persons we had harmed, and became willing to make amends to them all.

Step Nine We made direct amends to such people wherever possible, except when to do so would injure them or others.

Step Ten We continued to take personal inventory and when we were wrong, promptly admitted it.

Step Eleven Sought through prayer and meditation to improve our conscious contact with God as we understood Him, praying only for the knowledge of His will for us and the power to carry that out.

Step Twelve Having had a spiritual awakening as the result of these Steps, we tried to carry the message to others, and to practice these principles in all our affairs.

Adapted from Alcoholics Anonymous

Reference points for the journey

Serenity Prayer - attributed to Reinhold Niebuhr

God grant me the Serenity to accept the things I cannot change; Courage to change the things I can; and the Wisdom to know the difference. Living one day at a time; accepting hardship as a pathway to peace; taking, as Jesus did, this sinful world as it is, not as I would have it: Trusting that You will make all things right if I surrender to Your will; that I may be reasonably happy in this life and supremely happy with You forever in the next.
Amen

Operation Integrity Prayer

God, I pray that I will learn to desire obedience more than blessing or comfort and to know that the greatest blessing in life is to live obedient to Your will. May I learn to better give up my will and find my complete and total satisfaction in Your will. My self-centeredness destroys me but seeking You and doing Your will brings life to me. Realizing this, I have decided that my mind, my heart and my will, will be directed to You. I will find my purpose and identity in knowing You more personally & living more powerfully according to Your Spirit.
Amen

THE AUTHOR'S STORY

For years, I remembered little from my childhood, but I began to remember more and more as I grew in my early recovery. I remembered how my mother battled severe depression and mental illness, a battle she eventually lost to suicide. My father was a well-respected organist at church but also he had a secret stash of pornography which, as a young boy, I looked at whenever I could get away with it. My older sister suffered from eating disorders, and I was often in trouble with the neighbors or at school. When I was eight, a family friend from church took an interest in me. He took me fishing, to baseball games, and he began molesting me. Consistent with my family's pattern of secrets and shame, I never told anyone. I'm not sure which hurt me worse, being molested or thinking of how my father was cheating on my mom through his use of pornography.

By age nine I was exhibiting behavioral problems at school and church. The molestation continued and I continued to keep it secret. I was flunking school, barred from some after school activities, and often too disruptive for many Sunday School teachers. Finally, I was examined by a child psychologist and diagnosed mentally retarded. The doctors prescribed tranquilizers to control my behavior and I was placed in a school for mentally disadvantaged children. My name became "retard."

The people at the church my family attended said that God loved all the little children — yellow, brown, black and white. Had He forgotten about me? Was I some strange color, different from everyone else? I felt like people just wanted me to go away. Increasingly, I became defensive and competitive, determined to prove my own value. I prayed and pleaded for God to remember me — to help me. I remember sitting on my bed, in my adolescent years, reading *The Living Bible* and praying that somehow, someway God would give me a life that was useful and worthwhile. Silence.

In my early 20s, I was still attending church, but I had lost hope of ever having a life worth living. I began to drink. It started quite innocently; my first beer was with friends as we shared a pizza. I hated the beer taste but loved the warm feeling, the self-confidence and the sense of freedom the alcohol gave me. It was an answer of sorts. Within two weeks of that first beer, I was drinking everyday — heavily. Years went by, and I began to work weekends in a strip joint where I discovered cocaine, insane promiscuity and, along with the girlfriend I had at the time, I began to work in print and video pornography. Over the next five years, several of my friends were murdered and I saw numerous lives destroyed. I assumed that my life would be short, I feared for my own survival, but I was still unable to find a power that would change the way I felt about life.

In 1989, I moved to the West Coast vowing to start a new life. I started a business, made it successful, and began to religiously attend church once again. I smiled and pretended that life was great. But I was still utterly miserable. I never escaped thoughts of self-hatred and the feeling that everyone would be better off if I just went away. After a few years of abstaining from drugs and alcohol by sheer willpower alone, I periodically began to drink again and soon the drugs followed. Where I had previously been a daily cocaine user of generally small amounts, I now became a binge user of much larger amounts, adding crystal meth and heroin to the list of drugs used. I rationalized my drug use, saying I wasn't doing it every day. I convinced myself that I was entitled to have a little fun now and then.

In 1999, I went on what was to be my last drug binge. I had planned a little weekend getaway but I ended up traveling around Southern CA for three weeks, smoking $500.00 worth of crack cocaine every day, never eating or sleeping. During this trip, I overdosed three times, and three times I was arrested on felony drug charges. I would quickly bail myself out of jail after each arrest, and head back out on the road for some more of the same. I was not going to go home until I had some fun. I thought of it as recreation.

A few days later, when sitting in a seedy hotel, I called a friend named Bob, who I knew from church. Bob was a recovering alcoholic and drug addict who attended Alcoholics Anonymous and was very active at church. For the last few months I had been confiding to him about my drug use and my sense of hopelessness. I trusted him because it was obvious to me that, from his own experience, Bob knew the internal anguish I felt. And he was the only person I knew who seemed to really like being around me. During our phone conversation, Bob convinced me to stop drinking and doping for just that day and get some rest. And then later that night he drove for hours to pick me up and bring me home.

Once home, I got some very bad news. The State of California wanted me to go to prison for my drug crimes. It appeared that I had finally succeeded in destroying my life, even though I never meant to. However, following my attorney's recommendation I entered a drug and alcohol treatment program that combined counseling and the Twelve Steps as outlined by Alcoholics Anonymous. This program educated me about the reality of my addictions and confronted me regarding the destructive self-obsession behind most everything I thought and did. My drug life had been hell on earth, but this felt worse.

These early months in the program were preparing me for the greatest day of my life. That greatest day started with my attorney calling me in the morning to let me know things were not going well for me in the legal issues and that I should begin putting my affairs in order to serve my time in prison. Then that same afternoon, my counselor at the treatment program asked me to tell him about my personal belief in God. In response to his question, I recited to him by heart everything I knew about God from growing up in church and Sunday School. He listened for quite a while as I droned on and on, but then, with obvious frustration, he told me that he didn't want to hear any more. Surprised, I asked him why, and then he proceeded to tell me that I needed to find a real God and I needed to find a real Jesus. As you can imagine this offended me greatly and when I asked him why, he continued by saying, "Well, David, it is pretty obvious that the God and the Jesus that you think you have now hasn't done you much good. Has it?" When what he said finally sunk in to me, I sat stunned in silence facing the reality that whatever religious professions I had claimed had left me morally and spiritually bankrupt — void of the necessary power to live life successfully. I was more empty than empty.

Later that evening I was to meet my friend Bob, the one who picked me up and brought me home. He and I were going to discuss what needed to be done before I went to prison. It was dark and cold as I stood in an empty parking lot, alone and waiting for Bob to arrive. Looking up at the stars, I pondered the failure of my life and I began to pray. This was my life — I was $100,000 in debt, my family would not speak to me, my friends and business associates would barely tolerate me, I had overdosed on several occasions, and come close to being killed a few times. I was in a drug rehab and worst of all, all I really wanted at that very moment in time was more cocaine.

Standing there alone, I looked up at the stars and said, "Oh God! I am a drug addict and I don't even know who You are. I need help and I have nowhere else to turn. I am willing to call You by any name You want me to, but if You don't help me I am going to die."

At that moment, and for the first time in my life, I found a degree of personal honesty, the beginning of humility, and I accepted myself for who and what I was — a child in need. At that point, suddenly, everything in life seemed unimportant except for one thing — God. Either He would help me, or I was as good as dead. God was no longer just a "religious" belief; God was a life or death issue for me.

Standing there in the cold alone with nothing but my desperate prayer, I heard what seemed like a voice say, "Alright David, now I can go to work." Startled, I whirled all around looking for who had spoken to me. I looked behind the bushes next to the building to my left, and I looked under the cars which were to the right. I even looked inside the dumpster that was a few yards away. I looked all over that parking lot and there was no one there. It felt like I was going crazy, but I also sensed something big had just happened. Whatever had just happened, I knew my prayer had been heard and answered. I felt deep within me that things could be different for me in the future, that a new experience of life had begun. I had a sense that the battle for my life had been joined with power adequate to change what needed to be changed — me! For the first time I could remember, I knew I didn't have to be alone, and best of all, I had a real desire to live. By admitting that I was the problem, God gave me a solution. The solution was Him. That night in an instant, I became unconcerned about prison, unconcerned about what had happened to me in childhood; I was excited about life and I became ready to do all I could to fully experience the life God would make possible for me.

Ultimately, the court system had mercy on me, giving me the opportunity of long-term rehabilitation and probation. Motivated by a spiritual power deep within me, I continue to seek my Savior and He continues to do the work He promised to do — changing me from the inside out, guiding me and teaching me to surrender my will to His. As a result of His power, I have discovered wonderful gifts such as mercy, courage, love for myself and others, and hope. These gifts have enabled me to do things I have never dreamed of doing. I was baptized while attending my church's men's retreat, where I learned that for two years prior to my arrest a group of men had been praying for me. In God's world, I was loved even before I thought it was possible for me to be loved at all.

I am still receiving new and wonderful gifts today. My favorite one is gratitude for life — both past and present. My childhood misfortune and my addictions to alcohol, drugs and sex have become an important, and sometimes still difficult, part of what I believe to be a well scripted plan for my life. With the simple surrender of my will and life, which I don't always do, I continue to discover God in a loving and personal way. He is always willing to reveal Himself to me and to you as well. I now see that the story of my life has really very little to do with me. It has everything to do with God, and everything to do with you. For you see, it is my passion to tell others about the One who gives mercy and grace to addicted sinners like me. Because, if He gives mercy and grace to someone like me, then He will most certainly give it to anyone who sincerely asks for it. Any tragedy I have suffered and all comfort I receive is for the purpose of sharing with those who suffer so they can find comfort too. I have more blessing than I need.

Praise be to the God and Father of our Lord Jesus Christ, the Father of compassion and the God of all comfort, who comforts us in all our troubles, so that we can comfort those in any trouble with the comfort we ourselves receive from God.
2 Corinthians 1:3, 4 *TNIV*

WHEN LOST MEN COME HOME

It begins with a first step

CHAPTER ONE

We admitted we were powerless over our addictions, that our lives had become unmanageable.

—Step One from the Twelve Steps

No matter which way I turn, I can't make myself do right. I want to, but I can't.

—Romans 7:18 *NLT*

I am worn out from sobbing. Every night tears drench my bed; my pillow is wet from weeping. My vision is blurred by grief; my eyes are worn out because of all my enemies. Go away, all you who do evil, for the LORD has heard my crying. The LORD has heard my plea; the LORD will answer my prayer.

—Psalm 6:6-9 *NLT*

I am exhausted and completely crushed. My groans come from an anguished heart. You know what I long for, Lord; you hear my every sigh. My heart beats wildly, my strength fails, and I am going blind.

—Psalm 38:8-10 *NLT*

The End — The Beginning

I never wanted to be a sex addict. I never asked for it, and I certainly never intended it to take hold of my life the way it did. In fact, getting addicted to anything was the furthest thing from my mind. Nevertheless, addiction took root and grew in me, becoming entrenched into every fiber of my being.

The recovery process has helped me see how my destructiveness started when I was about eight years old. And I recognize that abuses I experienced in my early childhood, and my family history of addiction increased the likelihood of addiction in my life — and I could point fingers — but it does no good to blame anyone now. Learning the causes for my problems is helpful; learning to live free from my self-destructiveness is the truly important issue if I am going to live in a healthy way today and in the future.

Empowered in Powerlessness

Every day I realize how powerless I am — in my own power that is — to find the freedom that my soul longs for. Having said that, I do have days when I feel tremendous freedom, abandoning my old self-destructive ways and enjoying life's goodness to the fullest. There are other days, though, when I feel that at any moment I may catapult myself into a darkness that far exceeds my own ability to escape. Sometimes, sexual addiction assaults me with a conflict of mind, spirit and body, brutalizing me at the very core of who I am. Can you relate to this?

Those of us who have struggled with repeated patterns of sexually destructive behavior and who are honest with ourselves know this powerlessness, though we often have trouble admitting it. ***Recognizing and admitting personal powerlessness and insufficiency regarding an addiction is a fundamental principle that must be accepted deeply before anyone will find recovery and change for themselves and their life.*** Just like being an alcoholic, the solution starts with admitting we have a problem. Personally, I almost died in depression and shame before I accepted this simple truth. And I know of others who, even after countless failures, continue to claim confidence in themselves alone. It seems to me like they die a little more every day.

Without the benefit of honestly recognizing and admitting my addictions, my self-confidence was a liability to me. However, when I got honest about the true condition of my life, I could no longer avoid the reality of my sexual addiction. I could see that I was trapped in a progressing and accelerating downward spiral. My failures were personal and profound, born from the deepest places within me. My life was getting worse, never better.

STRENGTH IN NUMBERS

Each of us who participates in Operation Integrity has our own personal experience and story, but we celebrate together as one fellowship, a community of survivors who have an intuitive understanding of one another's experiences. And while our stories and experiences are all different, having unique patterns, behaviors and consequences, we see ourselves reflected in one another. This has taught us to focus on the similarities we share and not the differences. In this way we benefit individually from the total strength the fellowship offers as a whole. To the extent that we participate personally in our recovering community, we benefit from its resources. But it is more than this. Along with the benefits, we share the sufferings and shortcomings of one another at the same time. Anyone who wants to recover from sexual addiction is welcomed and accepted.

RECOVERY IS BOTH HARD AND SIMPLE

Addiction recovery is not fashionable, popular or exclusive. It is hard work and often marked by mishaps and mistakes. (At least that is how it has been for me.) The work of recovery is simple though. All that is required is an authentic desire to change, the courage to be honest and the willingness to do the work. And through personal experience, I've become convinced that the primary ingredient needed for recovery from sexual addiction is honest spiritual growth. Every area of a one's life must become re-oriented spiritually if life is going to be healthy and good for them.

As we seek God sincerely, and live transparently with others, we will be better able to face ourselves honestly and know **THE SOURCE** of power that leads us out of the darkness that ruled our lives in the past. When we are willing to face the honest facts about ourselves and take steps necessary to change, we discover an effective spiritual and personal life. We find a solution building and strengthening inside us. And with this strength we can become contributing partners with those around us. ***With the spiritual put in order, life's external struggles begin to resolve themselves with amazing simplicity.***

TRYING HARDER CAN MAKE THINGS WORSE

I grew up attending a large denominational church and many others in our fellowship maintained long and serious commitments to church and family. On the other hand, a number of us came from no particular religious faith; some even considered themselves agnostic or atheist when they first came to our fellowship.

Regardless of the religious position I claimed, my secrets, my addictions and my compulsions increased anyway. Destruction began to overtake my mind, my life and all that I was as a human being. More and more I became obsessed with the sexual conquest of women, focusing less and less on the important things in my life. I was increasingly obsessive about sex while working harder and harder to overcome the out-of-control way I felt about my life. Addiction was taking my mind away from me. Mentally, emotionally, and spiritually, I was being choked lifeless while I claimed to be in control. Repeatedly I made commitments to stop. But, I was losing touch with reality as I professed commitments and recommitments to God, to religious practice, to my family and to myself. I tried and failed again and again and again. No matter how much I tried, my best efforts always ended in failure. No amount of self-determination, effort or religious activity protected me from my addicted compulsions. No matter how hard I tried, I found no effective plan, method or power to permanently overcome my obsessions, or the shame that always followed them. The harder I tried, the worse things got.

How Addiction Starts

Addictions begin in subtle and seemingly benign patterns of behavior. And at first, no one is likely to notice. The compulsive behaviors related to sexual addiction are facilitated by internalized personal dynamics such as shame, embarrassment, loneliness, emotional isolation, mental exhaustion and a seemingly endless number of painful feelings anyone of us may experience. Virtually any pattern of emotional mismanagement and unhealthy behavior can initiate the growth of addiction, and by the time that most people suspect that they or a loved one is addicted in their sexuality, the addiction may be deeply rooted.

In my case, I tried very hard to make "good" use of my addictive inclinations. They entertained me when I was bored, comforted me when I was hurting, and they distracted me away from painful childhood memories as well as my chronic failures as a young adult. I rationalized them sincerely as harmless little pleasures, and at first I didn't suffer any destructive consequences. But deep within me I hated what I was doing. I worked desperately to stop my destructive behaviors, often slowing down or even stopping for a period of time. But all the while, addiction continued to grow inside of me quietly, silently gaining control.

Sexual addictions come from the deepest place within us, a place we can't reach on our own. In a very real way, our beliefs, our thinking, our feelings, our very selves are at the center of our addictions. With ineffective care and life management, anyone can become frustrated, resentful, fearful, dissocialized, and angry. We all at times feel abandoned, isolated, taken advantage of, having no sense of our true worth and value. It is within these dark and isolated places that sexual addiction finds ripe and fertile ground to take hold of us.

HOPELESSNESS RULED

Having lost the ability to stop my addictive behaviors permanently on my own, the only life I knew was a life of hopelessness. I had tried everything I knew to try and nothing had worked for me. I hated my behaviors and most of all I hated myself. Destruction grew inside me, and consequence grew around me, spilling over into the lives of others. Though I wanted to with all my heart, I could not stop the accelerating madness that characterized my life. At times I thought I had proven to myself that everything was going to be okay. But I was only deceiving myself, suffering one of the key hallmarks of addiction: denial, which is another way of saying, "I don't even know I'm lying." Also, ***denial of addiction is where we use seemingly rational and logical arguments to defy the addicted reality of our lives.*** In this way I marched self-willed, self-deceived and self-centered, unknowingly, deeper into my addictions, hating myself increasingly every step of the way, hoping and praying that everything would be okay, but fearing it would not be.

In the fellowship we share our stories with each other, how very often we could successfully (temporarily successful) bridle and contain ourselves, only to see our addicted compulsions ooze into other areas of our lives. Perhaps someone who used escort services and massage parlors would stop visiting them for a while and begin to believe he had conquered his problem. "Success" had been achieved, or so he thought; he was feeling great. Everything seemed fine, but sooner than later, he found himself living and behaving addictively in other areas of his life: alcohol, drugs or prescription medications, food, spending, gambling, work, and even the obsession of controlling the lives of others. The list of addictions is virtually endless; ultimately the results are the same.

Most all of us in one way or another substituted or rotated our addictions. This proved we were still addicts with dark secrets, toxic shame, and a laundry list of growing interpersonal failures. Our best efforts by themselves had changed nothing except the flavors and colors of our destructive patterns. Subconsciously, our addictions had become a permanent part of our lives. ***We were masters of ignoring the addicted reality of our lives, blind to see how we protected the addiction and denial that was destroying us.*** In rare moments of insight and clarity, we'd grasp the insane thinking behind our rationalizations, our minimizations and our excuses. But a moment later, we'd forget the pain our addictions created for us and others, thinking that all was well, that we were in control, and that we could have our cake and eat it too.

It seemed no matter how many times we hurt ourselves and others, we held on to the delusional belief that somehow, someway things would end differently the next time, opening the door to repeating the addictive cycle once more. Soon we were acting out again, always with the same result, a life of decay and personal demoralization. Insanity! Definition of insanity: *Doing the same thing over and over again and expecting different results.*

Reality is that any addiction that goes unnoticed or is not acknowledged by the one who is addicted will most likely intensify in obsession, frequency and duration. Addictions most always progress, although the addicted person usually doesn't realize it. Addictions simply outsmart people in this way. An immensely complex human phenomenon, addictions are fluid, odorless and colorless in all their forms. The pioneers of addiction recovery, Alcoholics Anonymous, assert that addictions are, "cunning, baffling and powerful." And they are.

Personally, I've found my own addictions to be very patient, hiding inside me and waiting to strike at the moment most destructive to me. Without fail, whenever I acted out in my addiction, my life and circumstances would begin to erode and my relationships would begin to suffer. Inside, I would feel as if everything good about me was being corrupted. There were times when I felt dead and spiritually I was. Quietly, inch by inch, I was being sucked dry of my dignity and my humanity. Evil wins every time when I pursue instant gratification and when it came to my sexual addictions, I was being robbed of and losing the most precious of God-given human dignities: my ability to make healthy and sane choices for myself.

In sharing with each other in the fellowship, we admit that we often felt victimized by those around us, but we really were just victimizing ourselves. Every day we fought harder and harder to hang on to the life we thought we wanted, and each day we lost a little more of our life, suffering injury every step of the way, always still fighting, and always still losing. ***We had been using our sexual behaviors as a way to escape from reality, but our escape had become our prison.*** When we experienced pain that seemed too much to handle, we resorted to our addictive acting out, and this increased our painful guilt and shame, which in turn created an increased likelihood of more destructive and severe acting out in the future. Caught up in this downward spiral, we were doing what the addiction demanded instead of what we truly wanted to do. Progressively, sexual addiction gave less and took more from us, even corrupting the personal values and priorities we professed. In one way or another, everything we said had become a lie. After a while no one believed us, but us. We were deceived, believing it impossible to stop even though we wanted to. At best, all we could honestly admit was that *we wanted to want to stop.*

In years prior to recognizing my own addicted condition, I had known others who suffered from very obvious addictions. Unable to relate to them because of my own denial, I would say things like, “Poor guy, too bad he never got his act together — better him than me.” Or, “Thank God I’m not like him. I can stop whenever I want to.” Or perhaps I had said, “I’m not like him, I’m only having a good time.” And of course, on numerous occasions I said, “I’m not hurting anyone.” These were my common thoughts of self-deception. And I believe many of us have shared these thoughts along with me. I was a master of rationalizing, minimizing and excusing, stubbornly denying the possibility that I was caught in the power of something bigger than me. I was just like the sad people I so righteously pitied, but I couldn’t see it.

At first glance it would have appeared that sexual addiction was my most dangerous problem, but it wasn’t. ***My most dangerous problems were the supporting denial and addiction to my own ego, my self-sufficiency and the belief that I was in control.*** Protecting my egocentric denial was the root problem that initiated, contributed to and maintained every addictive thought, desire and action I had. AA calls this *“self-will run riot, natural instincts gone awry.”* My life had become scripted by a warped sense of what I thought I needed and wanted, not about what was truly good for me. Furthermore, my commitment to control myself, my circumstances, and the lives of others in order to feel "okay" was killing me.

Our God-given instincts turn against us when we are dedicated to rule our own lives as if we were master of our own world. With an attitude like this, we lose sight of what we really need and want for our lives, blindly moving in a direction we don't really want to go.

I rationalized to myself because I couldn't explain my actions. I made excuses to others because I had no real answers for their questions. Being always committed to appear "normal" to others, I would hide my cries for help so those around me would only see the counterfeit image I felt I had to portray. Then, unable to live with my own self-deception, I would begin to think about the relief my addictions could bring me and I would return to what had poisoned me time and time and time again.

"Hell on Earth" is where the men of our fellowship have lived. And in our fellowship, we admit that the demands of our self-centeredness were too much for us and, we believed, too much for anyone else, too. Becoming ever more frantic, we looked for greater and more extravagant ways to prove ourselves acceptable to the world around us, hoping that someday, somehow we could truly believe in ourselves. We were fools and didn't know it! Does a fool ever know?

THE CRUSH OF SHAME

Sexual addiction will abandon you every time, always making you face the burden of shame and loss alone.

Here's how shame works: Shame brings misguided rules and regulations, a world of hiding and lies and make-believe with ruthless consequences for failure. Shame is an existence of personal condemnation. Shame makes us wonder if God regrets creating us. Shame makes us feel as if everyone else would be happier if we just went away. In shame we become our greatest judge, and addiction becomes our personalized form of self-execution. Shame erodes our bodies, our physical, emotional and spiritual health, making us feel mentally, emotionally and  spiritually sick. Shame causes us to prefer to be alone, and this  causes us to feel isolated and lonely most all the time. It's like shame moves in, contaminating us from the inside out. We try to make peace with ourselves but can't. Shame blocks our best efforts to heal and we stay stuck in self-loathing. In no uncertain terms we are, as it is written in the Psalms, "sick at heart" (Psalm 6:2 *NLT)*.

Our loved ones made repeated attempts to call us back with their love. But we ran. They were willing to make up the distance between us. But we ran further in shame. We promised them sincerely we would "straighten up." But sadly, after they repeatedly offered us love and understanding, which we so often rewarded with habitual deceit, our families and friends would begin to lose hope. Feeling abandoned and hurt, we would agree with them, feeling as though we were infectious somehow. It would feel like no one lived in our world and resentment would drive us further from our loved ones. Sometimes our friends and families had to make the decision to cut all ties with us for the sake of their own emotional survival. Who could blame them?

I wondered where God was. Why didn't He solve my problems? Why didn't He straighten me up? Why wouldn't He straighten me up? In my denial and shame, I had become an enemy to myself, and, unknowingly, at war with God and others as well. I was alone, desperate and dying and did not even consciously realize it. Many others have experienced this very same thing. Sometimes you'll know it, sometimes you won't.

> My disgrace is before me all day long, and my face is covered with shame at the taunts of those who reproach and revile me, because of the enemy, who is bent on revenge.
> Psalm 44:15, 16 *NIV*

Giving Up the Fight

Somewhere and somehow in the middle of my self-inflicted beatings, I finally gave up the fight. ***I became willing to relinquish my own personal idolatry***. Under the weight of all-consuming sadness, my personal foundations cracked. I admitted to myself that I was powerless over my sexual addiction and that my life was beyond my ability to manage on my own. In a moment of indescribable anguish and life-saving relief, I was broken. Amidst this ruthless and brutal reality, I experienced a new encounter with truth. I sensed that I was being confronted with the simple decision to surrender my right to my addictions, or to sink further and further and die. My abilities for choice had been reduced to only one: to live or to die. By admitting my own powerlessness over my addiction and my inability to manage my life on my own, I made a choice — a miracle in itself, really — a claim for personal honesty. And it was this choice that became the profound initial investment of honesty that was necessary to save and begin rebuilding my life. It was an investment that only I could make.

It's the way you've lived that's brought all this on you. The bitter taste is from the evil life. That's what's piercing your heart.
Jeremiah 4:18 *MSG*

Standing alone at the crossroad, I had nowhere to run or hide. What was it going to be — sexual addiction or life?

This truth-filled question, ugly as it was, became the seed of a new life for me. The surrendering of my stubbornness and my independence brought a new breath to my life and a light that opened my eyes so I could see what I needed to see. My honest

admission had made it possible for me to find what I needed to recover and live. ***Within this brokenness, I began to accept myself, my limitations and the truth of my failures.*** Though I did not realize it at the time, I had begun *the process* of joining the world as a whole person, one who was free to enjoy life as it was created to be.

The dignity to make a healthy choice for my life was returning to me even in this smallest way; my "wanting to want to" had begun to make sense. Somehow in my heart of hearts I knew that my repeated prayers had been heard. ***I had hit bottom, or perhaps, I had chosen to hit bottom.*** This had been my own personal Waterloo and I had lost. But in and through my loss, my life was being spared. The truth was now very clear to me. ***I do not have, and will never have, the dubious and sick luxury of self-deception!*** My humiliation had become a springboard toward humility.

No longer simply a sexual addict, I was becoming an honest sexual addict. A miracle had happened to me. And I was being prepared for greater miracles and better days ahead.

PERSONAL REFLECTIONS

PERSONAL REFLECTIONS

Seeing the dawn of hope

CHAPTER TWO

We came to believe that a Power greater than ourselves could restore us to sanity.

—Step Two from the Twelve Steps

All things are possible to Him who believes.

—Mark 9:23

Don't panic. I'm with you. There's no need to fear for I'm your God. I'll give you strength. I'll help you. I'll hold you steady, keep a firm grip on you.

—Isaiah 41:10 *MSG*

You can be sure that God will take care of everything you need, his generosity exceeding even yours in the glory that pours from Jesus.

—Philippians 4:19 *MSG*

FINDING REAL HOPE

While working to keep up my religious professions and church attendance, I struggled unsuccessfully to permanently stop using pornography which, in my case, promoted the use of alcohol and other drugs. In addition to alcohol, the drugs I used were cocaine and heroin, and I dabbled in methamphetamine on occasion. Finally, as is so often the case with those who use illegal drugs, I was arrested for my drug use and as an alternative to a prison sentence I was sent, fortunately, to a no-nonsense drug rehabilitation program. In this program I was monitored by urinalysis to make sure I was staying away from drugs, and I participated in group and individual counseling several times per week as required by the program. After about six weeks in the program, I was called into my counselor's office, a gentleman by the name of Bobby O.

Face to face, he sat right across from me and said, "David, you profess to be a Christian, right?"

"Yeah," I replied.

He then asked, "Would you please tell me about your Jesus; tell me about your God?"

So I went on to tell him everything I knew about Jesus and God. This amounted to a two, maybe three-minute historical accounting of what I had learned growing up in my church and Sunday School, the best I could remember it.

After a few minutes of patient listening, Bobby raised his hand to interrupt me and said, "Stop!" Then, looking me straight in the eye, he said, "David, I suggest that you find a new Jesus and a new God."

Feeling confused and quite offended, I asked him why.

And then, softly but very much to the point and once again looking me dead in the eye, Bobby said, "Well David, what you claim to know now hasn't done you much good, has it?"

Shocked and speechless, I was unable to respond to Bobby in any way that seemed to make sense. The words he said to me made me feel as if I was left without a body, like I was the hole in a donut, like my whole life had just been swept off the table and crashed to the floor in pieces. I had no defense. The truth Bobby O spoke to me was so utterly true that I could not attack it or even get mad at it or him for saying it. What he said made my religious pride and arrogance evaporate into the nothing it had always been. With my ball of religious yarn unraveled, it was painfully obvious that the impersonal religious instruction I had grown up with had actually blocked me from knowing THE TRUE GOD. And this is where my personal miracle began.

The anguish of that moment, and seeing my folly of misguided beliefs, opened my heart and my mind to know THE SOURCE OF POWER which had given me life — THE SOURCE OF POWER that had protected me patiently as I squandered my life — THE POWER that was now offering me the possibility of a life worth living. ***Seeking God starts with admitting how little we know about God.***

As absurd as it may sound, I believe that my addictions — the most core being my addiction to sex — are the second best thing that has ever happened to me. Somehow, while suffering the indignities that came from my addictions, a humble pliability took hold inside me. I was defeated inside and out. I'd had enough. I became desperate enough so that I was willing to try something new. I was ready to call on and trust something, SOMEONE bigger than me.

WHAT WORKS

In Step Two of the Twelve Steps, "came to believe" expresses open-mindedness and faith, the willingness to look in a new direction for the power and resources that make a difference in life. "Came to believe" also suggests that we bring ourselves physically and emotionally to be with others who are living  their lives with recovery and change successfully. We literally  replace the old environment(s) that have been part of our addictive cycles with new ones that help build healthy ways of living.

In my case, I "came to," — out of the addicted coma I had been living in for so long — and became consciously aware physically, intellectually and emotionally of the ugly reality that was my life. ***I "came to" realize that the only rational and reasonable thing to do was to look outside of myself, and let go of the self-centered belief that within myself I possessed everything necessary for a sane and healthy life. I "came to believe" that my only hope for a life worth living was to look beyond myself in order to find what was needed to make a difference in my life.***

In the Operation Integrity fellowship, we admit our struggles to one another often. We admit that we sometimes feel like we are disconnected mentally and emotionally. We realize and we admit that at all costs we must stay away from our addictions if we hope for a real and meaningful recovery and personal change. Remembering the suffering our addictions brought us and the fact we are powerlessness over our addictions keeps us moving forward in the right direction.

We also separated ourselves from the people, the places and the things that promoted our addictions. Following what our friends from Alcoholics Anonymous suggested, **"we became willing to go to any lengths."**

Getting free from our addictions didn't guarantee that life would be perfect, but to continue in the way we had been going almost certainly guaranteed our destruction. We had to gain some real integrity if life would ever improve. And together we are learning to have an authentic faith for recovery, which is to say we stop claiming faith only in ourselves.

On the occasions when we failed, which I did many times in my early recovery, we disclosed our failures honestly to one or more of our partners in recovery. This taught us we could regain some integrity simply by making an honest and open admission of our failures to someone who could understand our struggles. Amazingly, no one ever got tired of hearing about my failures. This is what a recovering fellowship is about — I am loved for who I am and who I am becoming regardless of my failures along the way. Recovery partners are more interested in me than my mistakes.

It was so bad we didn't think we were going to make it. We felt like we'd been sent to death row, that it was all over for us. As it turned out, it was the best thing that could have happened.
2 Corinthians 1:9 *MSG*

MOVING FROM HOPELESSNESS TO HOPEFULNESS

Almost every day, I found comfort within the fellowship of other recovering sex addicts, receiving support from those who've been wounded by life, then suffered and survived their own addictions. When I experienced the heartbreak of failure, they guided me from their own experience, helping me to feel a sense of hopefulness for my future and not the hopelessness I had felt in the past. They would tell me they felt themselves being strengthened every time they helped me. They would even thank me for calling them and asking for their help. ***In a real recovering fellowship, the weak get stronger and the strong get stronger by helping the weak.*** I experienced true faith for the first time in this way. It came to me before I knew it was even there.

Faith, as we experience it in Operation Integrity, is characterized by a hope-filled belief that compels us to take effective action. By understanding faith in this way, it becomes authenticated, making it an antidote for and the antithesis of addiction. Addiction kills our dreams, but faith gives hope for life.

Like a gift, the simple hope for life gave birth to a personal open-mindedness I had never experienced before. It appeared quiet and close, even before I asked for it, coming from outside of me, but working within. By seeing the changed lives of others I came to believe that I too could join them in freedom. My lifelong hopelessness had changed to hopefulness.

Relationship — Not Religion

Whatever I had previously thought I believed and then professed to others regarding God and/or religion didn't matter much because it obviously had not been authentic enough to really work for me. Others in the fellowship have experienced this same realization about their own religious beliefs and opinions. ***Those who claimed no God were in trouble and what others may have professed about God hadn't helped either. We all ended up in the same place — addicted.*** Call it whatever you want. What we really needed was real and effective help, and with an open mind and heart, we became ready to receive that help!

The concept of faith may offend those who consider themselves too smart to believe in God. For some, the mere mention of the word "faith" threatens self-indulgent egos and self-mastered lives. Some of our group had believed God was nothing more than a concoction of weak-willed people who were searching for answers through religious distraction and effort. And I agreed with them in one respect. Any "god" created within the mind of man is not God. ***Any "god" defined solely by human terms and descriptions serves only the dictates and demands of someone's predetermined thinking, which is to some degree, always flawed, shortsighted and ignorant.*** In these ways, whatever is believed cannot be God.

In a similar way, indifference, complacency, defiance, self-sufficiency and prejudice are in some ways understandable for those who, like me, were raised in religious environments that lacked nurturing love, were abusive or didn't affirm the human dignity God created within all people. We all suffer from pride and our own prejudices which block us from discovering God in a way that truly makes a difference in our lives. ***However, with hope for a new life connecting with the painful motivations created by our addictions, we realize we must seek God on His terms and not our own***. We must allow Him to tell us who He is and what He is all about.

REAL FAITH

Real faith is humble and willing to accept answers, any answer that helps us recover. A faith that hopes in a power greater than we are will not seek to debate, to conquer or win unnecessary arguments. ***In real faith we realize the need to live well is much greater than the need to be "right."*** Through a humble faith like this, the humiliation of sexual addiction can be molded into an openness which maximizes the chances for recovery and the restoration of a life truly worth living. In faith, we are transformed from victims to survivors, the kind of people who are able to help and guide others. ***Real faith is the catalyst of***

revolution for every man, be they religious minded or non-religious minded.

And faith is much more common than we may realize. Each of us exercises faith daily when we tap into the power of natural physics to make life more convenient. When you turn the key to your car, what do you expect? Power to start the engine. When you flip a light switch, what are you looking for? Light. What are you looking for when you pick up the telephone? To get connected. We have faith in the benefits of modern technology through personal experience. In the same way, we can learn faith in God by personal experience, too.

This is how I discovered a faith that gives me the power to recover from my addictions. In varying ways and with varying degrees of progress, I've discovered that I can trust in others, "higher powers" if you will, and The Higher Power, God.

So, if the thought of trusting God is troubling you, don't worry about it right now. There are lots of "higher powers" who can assist you in your recovery. ***Relax! And allow God to help you learn to trust Him. This, we believe, is the genesis of real faith after all.***

In our fellowship today, there are men who rejected God initially, but in their hope for recovery stayed open-minded. They made good use of other "higher powers" which helped them move into recovery, but only to the degree that they remained honest about themselves and open-minded about God.

The true "Higher Power" will reveal Himself to anyone who sincerely wants to know Him. Faith springs from hope for life. It flourishes from humility and honesty and openness, making us more and more aware of the goodness God seeks to give us. That's how it's been for me.

Faith is all about possibilities: the possibility that we can be restored to sanity, the possibility that we will truly gain freedom from our sexual addiction, the possibility that our personality and life will be changed and that God will be known in a personal and profound way. You don't need to know who to call for because when you call for THE TRUE GOD, He knows that you call for Him and only Him. There is no one else.

> "But there is One who has all power – that One is God. May you find Him now. Half measures availed us nothing. We stood at the turning point. We asked His protection and care with complete abandon."
> Alcoholics Anonymous, *The Big Book pg 59*

As we said before, some in our fellowship were very religious when they began their work of recovery. They asserted that their way of life was "the way," the "right way," or the "only way." But even with their powerful and prideful professions of faith, they became sexual addicts just like the rest of us. It was like their religious professions were more of a handicap, propping them up like religious scarecrows, empty and worn, unable to acknowledge and admit their needs and shortcomings. This is why it's so easy to hide in religion. I've done it personally many times and I've done it very well. The truth of the matter is this: while "religious" addicts maintain well-intentioned commitments, and may even speak eloquently about theology and God, their religious experience is contained within their own personal thinking and will never be sufficient for true spiritual living, as proven by their addiction. ***Sex addicts are sex addicts whatever their religion. And, religion by itself never cures an addiction of any kind. In reality, misguided rule-keeping religion promotes and deepens addiction, and can even become an addiction itself.***

True religion becomes reality only when it is relational, and part of a personal revolution that transforms someone — their thoughts, their feelings, their beliefs, and their actions. Anything less than this is not true faith or true religion. But, having said all of this, we don't encourage anyone to leave their church or denomination. Where we had failed to find a true personal faith and live it out in an honest and sincere religious experience, many others from various churches have succeeded.

Instead of trusting in our own strength or wits to get out of it, we were forced to trust God totally – not a bad idea since he's the God who raises the dead!
2 Corinthians: 1:9 *MSG*

So, is your *"religion"* working for you? Are your personal convictions successfully guiding you through life? Are you experiencing inside yourself the kind of life that keeps you free from the internal conflicts that result in addictions? If so, why are you reading this book? ***Addictions of any kind prove that we need to become spiritual where we have been pious, humble where we've been self-confident, honest where we've been self-deceived and open-minded where we have been stubborn.*** Before God will be anything to any of us, He will be our Savior. ***Either God is everything or He is nothing!***

When God touched me in His own time, I experienced a power that is deeply personal, beyond my comprehension and impossible to explain. New ground had been broken within me. God was revealing Himself in a way I had never imagined He would. And I hope the same for you.

"When I was driven to my knees by alcohol, I was ready to ask for the gift of faith. And all was changed. Never again, my pains and problems notwithstanding, would I experience my former desolation. I saw the universe to be lighted by God's love; I was alone no more.
Bill Wilson, *The Grapevine* January 1962

"In my own case, the foundation of freedom from fear is that of faith: a faith that despite all worldly appearances to the contrary, causes me to believe that I live in a universe that makes sense. To me, this means a belief in a Creator who is all power, justice and love; a God who intends for me a purpose, a meaning and a destiny to grow, however haltingly, toward his own likeness and image. Before the coming of faith I had lived as an alien in a cosmos that too often seemed both hostile and cruel. In it there could be no inner security for me."

Bill Wilson, *As Bill Sees It*

NECESSARY NEXT STEPS

In Operation Integrity, we believe that God and other "higher powers" can guide us back to sanity. Employers, parents, family, doctors, governments, law enforcement, each has power to control our behaviors. They are external powers who can influence our external behaviors in positive ways, and this helps change the way we think about our lives in a positive way. Listed below are some of the resources we found helpful to guide us in recovery and change our lives.

TWELVE STEP PROGRAMS AND SUPPORT GROUPS

We participated in Twelve Step support groups for sexual addiction. Sometimes we had other addictions and for those we attended the appropriate fellowship: Alcoholics Anonymous for alcoholics, Narcotics Anonymous for drug addicts, Gamblers Anonymous for gambling, Overeater's Anonymous for food addictions, and so forth. We followed the suggestion of ninety meetings in ninety days, staying away from our addictions between meetings. We read the literature and absorbed it, and asked for guidance from others in these fellowships. We sought time with other recovering addicts, who inspired us to see that we could experience recovery just as they had. We never stopped our Twelve Step meeting attendance, though the frequency of our attendance was adjusted as our addictions healed.

Sponsors and Mentors

We sought out a personal one-on-one relationship with a recovering sexual addict whose life exemplified spiritual renewal, someone who would be willing to guide and assist us at a deep personal level. We spoke to this person every day, maintaining our commitment to be fully honest and open with them. We followed their suggestions the best we could, realizing that their success would become part of our success only if we were willing to accept and follow the help they offered us. When given assignments by our sponsor, we did them the best we knew how. With our sponsor's help, we became proactive, which helped us to stay away from our addictions and guided us in building ongoing recovery and growth.

PROFESSIONAL CARE

Some of us were in need of rehabilitation programs. Getting appropriate professional assistance when needed is critical, so we took the opportunity whenever it was available to us. Also, we informed our personal physician of the nature of our addiction to ensure that we received appropriate care with the various possible side effects that accompany certain medications or treatments. Additionally, we sought out professional care through counseling, psychiatrists and psychotherapists. We found these compassionate people offered indispensable expertise by helping us see into ourselves and get to the honest truth of our lives.

HIGHER POWER — GOD AS WE UNDERSTOOD HIM

We asked for God's help, guidance and protection every day. In prayer, we admitted our distance from Him and that we suffered because we misunderstood Him and ourselves. In prayer, we began to see that God would meet us wherever we were, revealing His true nature and personality to us. Knowing that our addictions come from places deep within us, we asked God to touch us at the innermost place of our hearts and minds. And we discovered that God would do for us internally what others could only help us do externally. Ultimately, ***we came to realize***

that no external actions will change the internal, but internal changes will always change our external actions.

In the past, nothing had been more powerful than our addictions, but with God's help we could see this was going to change. Some of us felt that we had good reason to question God about the seeming inequities and unfairness about life. And so we did. Having honest questions and seeking honest answers from God is perfectly normal. Tough questions should never be ignored. Personally, I have found God always ready and willing to give real answers and real solutions when I am ready to listen and accept answers I may not like. ***Your Faith need not be perfect or without doubt to work.*** Be honest with God. Admit to Him the doubt you feel. Ask Him for His help. He will hear you. And He will help you.

Jesus said to him, "If you can believe, all things are possible to him who believes." Immediately the father of the child cried out and said with tears, "Lord, I believe, help my unbelief!"
Mark 9:22-23 *NKJV*

Medical professionals have told us that addiction is a learned and inherited disease. I call it the family dis-ease. It's progressive, incurable and even potentially fatal. ***I've also come to believe that addiction is the most human of all dis-eases; a phenomenon that reaches entirely across the human earthly experience.*** It destroys bodily health, soundness of mind, emotional well-being, and spiritual development. If a person develops a physical disease such as cancer, there are treatments that may cure the cancer. If there are mental or emotional difficulties, there are effective treatments through medication, psychotherapy and support groups. If you want to recover from sexual addiction, you'll have to address *all* of these with priority on the development of a personal and authentic spiritual faith. ***If you are willing to seek and discover the gift of spiritual renewal and wholeness, the physical, emotional and mental problems begin to heal as well.*** I know this from my own experience. I heal a little more every day.

So, you see, it is impossible to please God without faith.
Anyone who wants to come to him must believe that there is a
God and that he rewards those who sincerely seek him.
Hebrews 11:6 *NLT*

Personal Reflections

Decision that shapes destiny

CHAPTER THREE

We made a decision to turn our will and our lives over to the care of God as we understood Him.

—Step Three from the Twelve Steps

Teach me to do your will, for you are my God; May your good Spirit lead me on level ground.

—Psalm 143:10–11 *NIV*

Commit to the LORD whatever you do, and your plans will succeed.

—Proverbs 16:3 *NIV*

Listen for God's voice in everything you do, everywhere you go; he's the one who will keep you on track.

—Proverbs 3:6 *MSG*

A CHANGE OF HEART

I spent the first forty years of my life trying to overcome one thing or another, and failing most of the time. I tried to make good grades in school and make good decisions for my life, and to be a success in my work. But in one way or another I so often failed. When my best efforts ended up badly, I struggled and felt hopelessly abnormal and out of place. Just being me was painful and the pain I felt triggered powerful desires to escape what I was feeling, which opened the door to addictive temptations over and over again. This is how my addiction to sex slowly eroded the greatest of my God-given dignities: the ability to make clear and healthy choices for myself. My addictions always promised me so much, but they gave me less and less until, ultimately, they began taking from me. Time and again, they led me into deeper and darker forms of slavery.

But no more — things have now changed. ***Every day I stand at a crossroad.*** In one direction are the addictions that I have loved so much with their allure and destruction; in the other lies gut-wrenching openness and rigorous honesty. Sooner or later, we will all find ourselves standing here, and only honesty will enable us to know which way to choose.

The Most Significant Decision

Addictions diminish one's ability to make effective personal decisions. And as a consequence of our addictions we can also lose opportunities to make certain decisions. But, there is always one opportunity for choice that will forever be ours. ***What I do with my will is the single most significant and personal decision of my life. It can never be taken from me. I can never escape it. I am always responsible for it.*** We all have the opportunity to choose what our lives will be like, what kind of people we will be and who we will belong to. It's a simple decision that we face every day. Who will I trust? Who will I follow?

Always — or at the very least, most of the time — my intentions were honest, my goals seemed clear to me, and I absolutely never intended to become the kind of person who would make a disaster of one's life. But I did. My personal willpower and ambition not only abandoned me, but also propelled me to become a prisoner to the very things I once felt entitled to. My addictions cost me the mental clarity I needed to make certain specific choices, and they caused the loss of opportunities to make others.

The decision to surrender myself to God's care is a different kind of decision — one that is far more personal and practical than religious. I surrender my will and life to God and

 His care or I continue as I was and die. ***God is a life-and-death decision for all of us.*** In one way or another, and sometimes without consciously realizing it, we all decide whether we are willing to trust God or continue our journey alone. Personally, I recognize that failing to trust God with my life leaves me spiritually alone and unprotected against my own progressing addictions — a potentially fatal mistake for any addict. 

No Hand-Me-Down Faith

There is no such thing as "hand-me-down faith." Ultimately, every one of us will stand before God with our future literally in our own hands, deciding for ourselves what kind of person we will be and what our life will stand for. Some of the men in the recovery group I attend, when they made their decision to entrust themselves to God, experienced immediate and profound gratitude with dramatic emotional outbursts. Others experienced only a quiet sense of relief that their life would change for the better. Whatever the experience, each of us knew it was far better to make the decision to surrender and trust than continue on the way we were going. It was very simple, really; we could no longer trust ourselves to manage our lives alone.

Trust in the Lord with all your heart; do not depend on your own understanding. Seek His will in all you do and he will direct your paths.
Proverbs 3:5-6 *NLT*

Everyone is affected by external influences. We are influenced by our social environments, by our friends, our families and our coworkers. And we are commonly identified by our appearance, profession, and social status. While our external circumstances may appear to be the most dominant aspect of our lives, it is really our will that is the true center point of every man and woman.

My will is always central to who I am and who I will become. Behind everything I say or do is my will. It is the doorway of decision through which I give and take in this world. The will is what initiates and dictates the actions of one's life. ***The will is where the one and only real question of life is asked: Will you be self-directed? Or, will you be God-directed?***

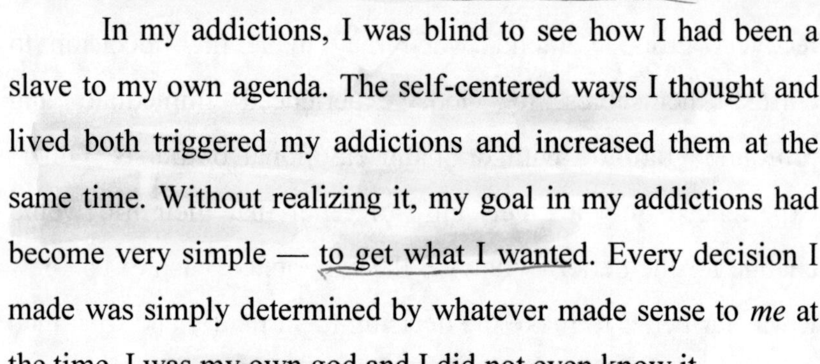

In my addictions, I was blind to see how I had been a slave to my own agenda. The self-centered ways I thought and lived both triggered my addictions and increased them at the same time. Without realizing it, my goal in my addictions had become very simple — to get what I wanted. Every decision I made was simply determined by whatever made sense to *me* at the time. I was my own god and I did not even know it.

So, in order to find a new and better way to live, I had to make a new decision. And in making this new decision I also made a new goal. My new goal is to ask — continually ask — God to manage and care for that part of me that is made in His image. The part of me that is personally unique: my will. My goal then became the pursuit of an honest and open relationship with God. To a sex addict like me, anything else is death.

We had to quit playing God. It didn't work. Next, we decided that hereafter in this drama of life, God was going to be our Director. He is the Principal; we are His agents. He is the Father, we are His children. Most good ideas are simple, and this concept was the keystone of the new and triumphant arch through which we passed to freedom.
Alcoholics Anonymous, *The Big Book pg 62*

God, I offer myself to Thee – to build with me and to do with me as Thou wilt. Relieve me of the bondage of self, that I may better do Thy will. Take away my difficulties, that victory over them may bear witness to those I would help of Thy Power, Thy love, and Thy way of life.
May I do Thy will always!
Alcoholics Anonymous, *The Big Book pg 63*

Don't copy the behavior and customs of this world,
but let God transform you into a new person,
by changing the way you think.
Romans 12:2 *NLT*

Once I made the decision to turn my will over to God's care, I quickly learned that it is impossible to do this without turning my life over to God's care as well. We simply cannot do one without the other. ***This is because the way we live our lives is the truest indicator of our will, and until we are willing to give our life to God entirely, we have not surrendered our will, either.***

My problem had been that I had considered my personal wants and wishes as if they were necessities, making demands in ways I was not even aware of. I wanted my way and I wanted others to agree, cooperate and assist me in obtaining what I wanted, with little regard for the impact on others. When I failed to get what I wanted, I became angry and resentful, which proved just how selfish my motivations really were at the time, regardless of how good I thought my intentions were. And often, without realizing it, I would punish others in one way or another, and in so doing, I became intolerable to an extent that those around me would leave me or reject me. Then, my misery would grow all the more, making my addictive inclinations seemingly irresistible once again.

Are you like I have been? Are you at odds with the world and the people in it? Sometimes, with very little provocation, we can be like mercenaries. We fight to get what we think is important. If pushing and shoving doesn't work, we "kill 'em with kindness" to hide our selfish motives. We sometimes claim victory. And other times we politely admit defeat — faking surrender — in order to regroup and try to win once again.

TRUE SURRENDER

In true surrender to God, we quit fighting anyone or anything, because we know the only battle really worth fighting is within ourselves. Because I am powerless over people, places and things, it is essential that I keep as my primary goal a faith that longs for God and trusts in His care. A trusting relationship with God always brings improving character.

"You know you're surrendered to God when you rely on God to work things out instead of trying to manipulate others, force your agenda, and control the situation. You let go and let God work. You don't have to always be 'in charge.' Instead of trying harder, you trust more."
Rick Warren - *The Purpose Driven Life*

Sexual addiction can be like a train wreck. Just because we put on the brakes does not mean we won't crash and have the pieces of our lives come apart. Consequences already set in motion by poor decisions and destructive actions will likely play themselves out to their natural conclusion. How we come to accept the world, our circumstances and our consequences varies individually, but the willingness to accept the things we cannot change is essential. ***True surrender means being willing to accept the world and the circumstances that are beyond our ability to control.*** This is essential for everyone, addicted or not.

As I recover and grow, I am learning to make peace with an imperfect and often unfair world. It's broken and it just doesn't run right. I see others getting away with things I no longer get away with but wish I could. At the same time, I find myself asking — or maybe it's God asking me — How many times did people look at the way I lived and wonder why I was getting away with those same things? The truth is no one gets away with wrongdoing. Sooner or later, we all reap what we sow.

Regardless of the difficulties I face in this world, it is my job to focus on my spiritual relationship with God as I understand His will to be, and allow others to do what they will, be it right or wrong. A man's freedom is his right according to his Creator. ***God gives every man the right to make his choices. It's not our place to judge.*** By virtue of the gift of recovery, my response-ability is to do all I can to make my life right with God and with others. This I can do.

It Is a Process

Having faith in God empowers me to accept a 'process' way of life for others and myself. We are all in process. My process is my job, not yours. Your process is your job, not mine. We have little or no control over anything except our own willingness which is the key to unlocking a life changing recovery. I am entrusted by God with my opportunity for my life, whether I lose it or find it restored. ***I am not called to be successful. I am called to be faithful. With this simple attitude, I am able to make a positive contribution to the world around me.***

God, grant me the serenity to accept the things I cannot change,
the courage to change the things I can,
and the wisdom to know the difference.
Serenity Prayer

This life therefore, is not righteousness, but growth in righteousness, not health but healing, not being but becoming, not rest but exercise. We are not yet what we shall be, but we are growing toward it: the process is not yet finished but it is going on. This is not the end but it is the road; all does not yet gleam in glory but all is being purified.
Martin Luther

"I know the plans I have for you", says the Lord. "They are plans for good and not for disaster, to give you a future and a hope. In those days when you pray I will listen. If you look for me in earnest, you will find me when you seek me. I will be found by you," says the Lord. "I will end your captivity and restore your fortunes. I will gather you out of the nations where I sent you and bring you home again to your land."
Jeremiah 29:11-14 *NLT*

GRACE

I know God loves all people including those of us who became addicted sexually. God not only loves you, He delights in you and wants you no matter who you are or what you have done. I am convinced of this because I have discovered it for myself. He reveals himself to me through the opening door of my honest, open and willing surrender. Thankfully, ***having an authentic relationship with God is not a matter of how smart I am, but how sincere I am with Him.*** He takes care of the rest. It's simple, it's effective and it's called grace. Grace is God's gift of a new life, no matter who you are, where you are or what you have done. God is concerned for you and He reveals himself to anyone who is interested in Him. When you are ready to receive and accept it, God's grace will always be there to meet you. He'll make His home in your heart. From there He will move into every aspect of your life, continually expanding His presence and filling you with Himself.

I believe all people — whether they know it or not — intuitively long for a spiritual and eternal Father, one who knows exactly what they need, one who is eternally committed to love and care for them perfectly. We all need an authentic relationship with a perfect Father. And this is where Jesus comes into the plan for our redemption. Jesus is the One Person who has always known God as the Perfect Father. He reveals who God the Father is and what God the Father is like. ***God may never be exactly what we want Him to be, but He will always be everything we need Him to be.*** There has always been only one whose life displayed perfection of purpose, whose death exemplified the perfection of love and who lived again after death, proclaiming the perfection of power that altered the course of world history and changing individual lives.

In Jesus, I experience someone whose destiny offered Him all privileges but — by His own choice — gave up His entitlements, preferring to love others in surrender and obedience to God his Father. He embraced those who admitted their need for Him, anyone who was willing to ask for His help. He forgave those who sought to destroy Him. He never retaliated, nor defended Himself. He expressed love for those who killed Him, because He knew they did not understand who He was or what He was about. After giving up His life, He lived again and appeared to His followers, proclaiming once and for all His role as The One who is capable of giving life to dying men. He chose to associate with those who, like me, were socially and personally ravaged, drawing us to Himself, to His love and to His Father.

I am empowered by Jesus Christ according to His power and the gift of faith I have in His power. It is in Jesus that I have life and confidence in God's care. Thank God Jesus loves the sexually addicted like me.

This is how much God loved the world: He gave his Son, his one and only Son. And this is why: so that no one need be destroyed; by believing in him, anyone can have a whole and lasting life. God didn't go to all the trouble of sending his Son

merely to point an accusing finger, telling the world how bad it was. He came to help, to put the world right again. Anyone who trusts in him is acquitted; anyone who refuses to trust him has long since been under the death sentence without knowing it. And why? Because of that person's failure to believe in the one-of-a-kind Son of God when introduced to him.
John 3:16-18 *MSG*

The man and the life of Jesus can never be contained in a history lesson or a theological discussion. ***The only place for Him and His Spirit to be is in the lives of men and women who, like me, become infused with His Power as a result of their faith and hope in Him.*** His life is my life. His God is my God. My life is His. God does not exist for me. I exist for God. *Looking through the lens of eternity, everything begins to make sense.* I am increasingly aware of the joy God brings, His excellent plan for me and the assurance that my life, the world around me, and the universe as a whole are loved by Him completely. The love of Jesus is changing my heart and as my heart changes, my mind is changing too. *The recovery I am receiving is not about rule-keeping, religious moralizing and self-imposed corrections.* I have experienced a complete change of allegiance, now preferring an intimate relationship with God above my sexual addictions, above my life, above everything. Jesus lived courageously, died lovingly and lived again eternally so we can know that God eternally forgives you and me. Are you ready to say…?

Dear God, I pray that I will learn to desire obedience more than blessing or comfort and to know that the greatest blessing in life is to live obedient to Your will. May I learn to better give up my will and find my complete and total satisfaction in Your will. My self-centeredness destroys me but seeking You and doing Your will brings life to me. Realizing this, I have decided that my mind, my heart and my will, will be directed to You. I will find my purpose and identity in knowing You more personally and living more powerfully according to Your Spirit. Amen

The Operation Integrity Prayer

Personal Reflections

Knowing the landscape prevents a fall.

Chapter Four

We made a searching and fearless moral inventory of ourselves.

—Step Four from the Twelve Steps

Let us examine our ways and test them, and let us return to the Lord.

—Lamentations 3:40

Complain if you must, but don't lash out. Keep your mouth shut, and let your heart do the talking.

—Psalm 4:4 *MSG*

Stay alert; be in prayer so you don't wander into temptation without even knowing you're in danger. There is a part of you that is eager, ready for anything in God. But there's another part that's as lazy as an old dog sleeping by the fire."

—Matthew 26:41 *MSG*

Say Hello to You

Sexual addiction is about escape. The addictive acting out we have done made it possible for us to temporarily avoid uncomfortable and painful feelings like inadequacy, fear, hopelessness, loneliness and the feeling of being unwanted or unloved. But we could not escape these painful feelings forever. Sooner or later they always returned, usually with a vengeance. And, because most of us grew up having painful feelings we could not escape, we may have grown callused to them, and not realized we felt like we did. We often even trained ourselves subconsciously to avoid our feelings through thoughts, fantasies and other intoxicating experiences, thereby losing connection with what was really going on inside us. It's like we had unknowingly developed our own world of make-believe and become lost in it. But this will never work for long. Anyone who wants to recover will have to leave their fantasies behind them, and accept the real truth of who they are and the reality of their lives.

Making an inventory of our feelings, beliefs, attitudes and actions is a pursuit of this reality. It is a commitment to recognize and acknowledge one's personal truth, so that our wounds can be healed. Personally, I would have much preferred to do someone else's inventory, but I was the one who needed recovery, so I stuck with taking inventory of myself. It was not fun and it was not easy.

Have You Been Fooling Yourself?

You cannot become the person God created you to be if you play games with the truth. To make a real claim for the kind of faith that leads to recovery, it is your responsibility to pursue self-clarity, so you can learn to understand who you are, what you are about, why you think the way you do and why you do the things you do. This may even mean admitting how hopeless you still feel, or how weak you feel your faith to be. ***If we want to know God personally, the place to start is with the truth about ourselves.***

God is a God of truth. He is a God of reality. To procrastinate in this work of self-honesty is to avoid the process of growing in relationship to God, who is our only hope. All God is asking you to be is completely honest — right now. With your addiction as obvious evidence, you were not honest in the past, and tomorrow may never come. Your opportunity for recovery is to face yourself honestly, today and every day. Procrastination is deadly to sexual addicts.

The moral inventory is a cool examination of the damages that occurred to us during life and a sincere effort to look at them in

true perspective. This has the effect of taking the ground glass out of us, the emotional substance that still cuts and inhibits.
Bill Wilson, *As Bill Sees It*

You want me to be completely truthful, so teach me wisdom.
Psalm 51:6 *NCV*

There is no effective substitute for a truthful, realistic perspective of who you are. Honesty, openness and willingness — the very things we run from in our addictions — are required. Most everyone in Operation Integrity will readily admit they felt fearful and reluctant about making their own personal inventory. It can seem like an impossibly uncomfortable thing to do. We all needed help. Being open-minded, we were willing to ask for the help we needed. And we got it. We got help from our sponsors, our mentors and our counselors. If you need help, ask for it. You are not alone.

Willingness Expressed Through Action

Real willingness — always expressed in diligent action — is absolutely indispensable. By honestly recognizing our need for help and open-mindedly accepting help from others, we willingly display the kind of fortitude that is needed to continue our work of recovery. Recovery requires courage. ***Courage is the objective willingness to move forward in spite of our fear – to move in the very direction in which we are afraid.***

When you made the decision to turn your will and your life over to God, you became a partner with Him, partnering to develop His miraculous purposes in your life. Now, doing your personal inventory is your partnership 'response-ability.' No one can do this but you. While we are doing our work, God helps our hearts trust and our minds to think in healthier, more productive ways.

"It is not your diligence; it is not your examination of yourself that will enlighten you concerning sin. Instead, it is God who does all the revealing... If you try to be the one who does the examining, there is a very good chance that you will deceive yourself."
Jeanne Guyon

God is in charge of human life, watching
and examining us inside and out.
Proverbs 20:27 *MSG*

The first step toward fortitude is dissecting our fears to find out what it really is that we're afraid of, then asking ourselves, is this fear legitimate? When we take the time to look at our fears in this way, most often we'll find that the fear overlooks God's active presence. If the fear is one of loss, remind yourself of God's promised provision. If the fear is one of ridicule, thank God you have an opportunity to grow in humility! Remind yourself that nothing can happen to you apart from God's watchful care. He doesn't blink, and He can use any circumstance for His good.
Gary L. Thomas, *The Pursuit of Glory*

He is working in you. God is helping you obey Him.
God is doing what He wants done in you.
Philippians 2:13 *NLT*

Sexual addiction is not the cause of our moral failings nor is sexual addiction a moral failing in and of itself. Sexual addiction and the subsequent moral failings are the result of spiritual and emotional malnourishment. When making a moral inventory we sift through our past and present behaviors in order to recognize selfish thinking, misguided or inaccurate beliefs and the ineffective emotional developments that promoted our addictive behavior. ***It is essential that we see these things for what they really are, so they can be changed or eliminated from our lives. A man's hidden nature creates his external actions, and moral failings will continue if they are not faced and dealt with honestly***.

You are so careful to clean the outside of the cup and the dish,
but inside you are filthy – full of greed and indulgence! You
Pharisees! First wash the inside of the cup, and then the outside
will become clean, too.
Matthew 23:26 *NLT*

Making my personal inventory helped me to see specific things in me that promoted my addictive thinking and acting. I was able to see how self-centered I was, how lonely I was, how angry I was and how frustrated I had been most of my life. My personal inventory was a practical, measurable commitment to clear the ground in preparation for the construction of a new person made by the design and resources of God, The Master Builder of Life. Gaining increased objectivity about myself in this way set me on course to bring my heart and mind together in agreement with God. No longer alienated spiritually from God and from myself, I sensed I was becoming a member in the family of the most blessed of all men.

"If we are painstaking about this phase of our development, we will be amazed before we are halfway through. We are going to know a new freedom and a new happiness. We will not regret the past nor wish to shut the door on it. We will comprehend the word serenity and we will know peace. No matter how far down the scale we have gone, we will see how our experience can benefit others. That feeling of uselessness and self-pity will disappear. We will lose interest in selfish things and gain interest in our fellows. Self-seeking will slip away. Our whole attitude and outlook upon life will change. Fear of people and of economic insecurity will leave us. We will intuitively know how to handle situations which used to baffle us. We will suddenly realize that God is doing for us what we could not do for ourselves."

Alcoholics Anonymous, *The Big Book pg 83-84*

FOCUS ON YOUR INVENTORY

During this process, you may find yourself obsessing over damage done to you by other people. I admit I did on many occasions. Others may have caused profound harm to you, but for now, it is essential that you concentrate on your own mistakes, and not on the mistakes of others. This is your inventory, no one else's. You are responsible for your recovery and changing your life. Let others work out their own problems with God just as you and I are doing. Their personal problems are not our job and certainly none of our business. Any resentment you have should be listed and cataloged as part of your inventory. You can discuss them with your sponsor or mentor at the appropriate time.

My recovery partners and I approached our personal moral inventories in different ways. But there were some common characteristics. We each faced some tough questions posed to us by our sponsors and other people who were helping us in our recovery. Then we wrote about ourselves in journals, noting our responses to the questions asked. Personally, I found recovery workbooks quite helpful. We wrote about our family history and any memories of our families which we thought were important, writing down every thought, memory and feeling the best we could. We wrote about the people who harmed us. We wrote about the people we harmed. We wrote a great deal about our sexual experiences, why we did the things we did, and how we felt when we were doing them, and how we felt after doing them. We wrote about love, what we desired for love to be like and how we may have been disappointed by those we loved. We wrote it all. We wrote everything. Here are some of the questions that we asked ourselves:

- What are you angry about and why?
- How have others hurt you?
- Who hurt you? Was it parents, family members, people from church or school, neighbor, enemy, friend?
- What or whom are you afraid of?
- Do you remember your first sexual experience? What was it?
- How old were you when you began the behaviors that turned into your sexual addiction?
- How have you violated your own sexual ethics?
- When did you first think you may be addicted sexually?
- How have your sexually addictive behaviors increased over time?
- How have you violated or objectified others sexually, personally or socially?
- How have your sexually addictive behaviors impacted your spouse, your children, your health and your career?
- How have you violated or objectified yourself?
- How have you abused those weaker than you?
- How have you been greedy?
- How have you been selfish?
- How have you been a hypocrite religiously, sexually or socially?

- How have you expressed unwarranted pride?
- How have you manipulated others and your own thinking through self-pity?
- When and why do you feel self-pity?
- Why are you willing to sacrifice long-term health and sanity for short-term gratification?
- How and why have you minimized your mistakes and addictions?
- How have you exaggerated your successes?
- Have you minimized your successes? Why?
- What do you like about yourself?
- What do you not like about yourself?
- What do others like about you?
- How have you blamed others for your difficulties?
- What do you feel guilty about?
- Is there anything that you are intentionally avoiding? What is it?
- Are you, or about what are you procrastinating regarding your inventory?
- Why do you lie?

I spent about a week, working every day, setting aside a specific time each day to do my work. Daily, I asked God to help me to move through whatever fear and trepidation I was feeling at the time. It helped me to start with recent events and the things that were most troublesome to me. The more I wrote, the more I remembered and the more clarity grew within me. After a few days I actually began to enjoy the experience of making my inventory. I certainly wouldn't say it was fun, but the working commitment to my own recovery coupled with a sense of courageous accomplishment produced gratitude within me.

As I honestly answered these kinds of questions, I found myself becoming more open to God, and having a strength I had never known before. Amidst my honest open and willing search, God was making it possible for me to address and begin resolving my issues once and for all. ***I had a sense that my failures and shortcomings could now be rehabilitated, reinvested and transformed into wonderful assets.***

If you sense anger when writing, write about it. If you sense fear, write about it. If you feel resentment, write it down. Write everything down so that your sponsor/mentor and counselor can talk it over with you — face-to-face. ***We don't need to be perfect by any means, but we do need to do the best we possibly can.***

As we learn to understand the real facts about ourselves, we begin to grasp a real worldview of who we are and how we have hurt ourselves and those around us. And this makes us ready to change. We also begin to let our resentments go, realizing that, with God's help, it's possible that we can forgive every person who has hurt us, starting with forgiving ourselves. Resentment kills sex addicts. In forgiveness, we release ourselves from the hurts others caused us. And, procrastination delays the forgiveness that leads to freedom. This is why lollygaggers don't recover from sexual addiction.

> To forgive is to set a prisoner free, and to
> discover all along the prisoner was you.
> Corrie ten Boom

Personal Reflections

A journey shared

CHAPTER FIVE

Admitted to God, to ourselves and to another human being the exact nature of our wrongs.

—Step Five from the Twelve Steps

Confess your sins to one another and pray for each other so that you may be healed.

—James 5:16 *NLT*

He who conceals his sins does not prosper, but whoever confesses and renounces them finds mercy. Blessed is the man who always fears the LORD, but he who hardens his heart falls into trouble.

—Proverbs 28:13-14 *NIV*

Since we've compiled this long and sorry record as sinners (both us and them) and proved that we are utterly incapable of living the glorious lives God wills for us, God did it for us.

—Romans 3:23 *MSG*

GETTING REAL WITH OTHERS

For forty years I lived in isolation. Raised in a large metropolitan area surrounded by thousands, if not millions of people, I learned to exist alone in the world. I had grown to prefer my life that way because I had never known any other way. It was the way of my family. The rule in my family was that weakness, when exposed, would be ridiculed, if not punished. And from this example, I grew up believing I was entitled to my selfishness as long as I kept it veiled behind a veneer of politeness, civility and "christian" respectability. By the time I was an adolescent, I was a master of avoiding my problems and any people or situations that could expose my shortcomings or the loneliness I felt inside. I feared others. I doubted my worth. I had no confidence in my upbringing. I survived and existed. My life was a living hell.

I was 41 years old when I got help from others and began stopping my addictions, which was a big step in the right direction. But, in addition to stopping my destructive way of life, I also needed to learn how to come out of the isolation I had learned as a child, to live in a real world of real people, and have real relationships with them. I'm not sure which felt worse: the painful experience of detoxing from drugs and alcohol or the experience of getting honest about myself with others.

A New and Better World

My part in the recovery process required me to become more honest with myself, God and other people. This was a slow and difficult process, but as I did it, I began to experience a new closeness with friends and a respect for myself that I had never had before. This new way of relating to others felt strange in the beginning, but it also felt good. It was like I was being baptized into a new and better world. ***By admitting my faults and vulnerabilities to people who could understand and empathize with my experience, I was able to rise above the sense of condemnation I learned as a child.***

The 'getting honest' part of my recovery work transformed my self-disgust into a compassionate regard for myself and my own life experience. ***Allowing other people to know my mistakes and vulnerabilities helped me experience the relational acceptance I needed.*** Listening without judgment or criticism, they modeled to me the grace and acceptance I didn't get at home. This lightened the burden of shame and guilt I felt, which encouraged me to become even more honest still. But there was more to this experience. I started to feel lightness in my heart, and even, at times, found humor in the things that once threatened my health and my safety. I could accept and laugh at myself like never before. I was on a new path which was leading me out of isolation and fear of the past to a newfound sense of wholeness and honest friendship with others. This honest and transparent way of recovery brought me authentic, burden-bearing friendships I previously thought were not going to be possible for someone like me.

"You're blessed when you're content with just who you are – no more, no less. That's the moment you find yourselves proud owners of everything that can't be bought."
Matthew 5:5 *MSG*

SAYING GOODBYE TO SECRETS

When we are ready to accept the grace God and others have for us, our secrets become like broken kindling which help build warming fires of joy and comfort for us and those around us. Isolation becomes joyful fellowship. It is replaced with relational assurance and confidence. Not like the temporary, intoxicating feelings our addictions gave us, but a deep, profound sense of goodness, openness and oneness with God and the world He created. When we say goodbye to our secrets, we become honest and free men. We grow to become more like Jesus.

We hide what we know or feel ourselves to be (which we assume to be unacceptable and unlovable) behind some kind of appearance which we hope will be more pleasing. We hide behind pretty faces which we put on for the benefit of our public. And in time we may even come to forget that we are hiding, and think that our assumed pretty faces is what we really look like.

Simon Tugwell, *The Beatitudes: Soundings in Christian Traditions*

For me, admitting my faults was like a desperate grasp for life, because the life I had been building with my secrets had been killing me. For others in Operation Integrity, it was more of a powerful claim for personal freedom. In either case, it is a breaking away from the secrets and addictions which deceived and buried us ever deeper into a world of increasing self-deception and isolation. Getting real with God and another person is an opportunity to receive supernatural help and human assistance together. It is our personal way of reaching out, revealing ourselves — confronting, exposing and then ultimately accepting the faker-impostor that's lived inside of us. Allowing others to know us thoroughly brings us into humble alignment with God, Who will delightfully breathe life into the true and honest person we hope to become. ***By getting real and being honest, we make ourselves available to be loved.***

ALIGNED TO TRUTH

The purpose of admitting our wrongs to God isn't to enlighten Him by filling in the gory details of our life, as if anything were a surprise to Him. After all, He knows the whole story better than we do. When we admit the exact nature of our wrongs to God, we consciously and purposefully bring ourselves into agreement with God, Who is our Hope for Life. ***We accept the facts of our lives just as they are without argument, aligning ourselves with God and His Truth.*** This our right place before God, our right place in His universe. Where before, we had aligned our lives with self-rule, deception and secrets, we now align ourselves with God's truth, and this leads to the recovery of our heart, soul, mind and our true strength as men and women of freedom. Ultimately, no one escapes the truth, but by admitting the truth about ourselves we move toward the wholeness we have been searching for all of our lives. We are simply taking the "bull by the horns" and taking responsibility for our lives and our future. ***Which is better — to die with secrets and then face our Creator in arrogant deception, or to seek Him now and humbly reveal ourselves, which is a way we ask for mercy? God gives real mercy to real people. If we want life, mercy and life, we have got to get real.***

> The time is coming when everything will be revealed; all that is secret will be made public. Whatever you have said in the dark

will be heard in the light, and what you have whispered behind closed doors will be shouted from the housetops for all to hear!
Luke 12:2, 3 *NLT*

My false and private self is the one who wants to exist outside the reach of God's will and God's love – outside of reality and outside of life. And such a self cannot help but be an illusion.
Thomas Merton in James Findley's, *Merton's Place of Nowhere*

In the past, we used self-deceit and manipulation of facts much like Adam and Eve used fig leaves to avoid exposure. But to live, we step out from our hiding places and reveal our naked vulnerability. We make ourselves accountable for our lives, and trusting in God's mercy and care, we become ready for God to reveal His loving and compassionate nature to us. Our movement toward God is in response to the call He's been making to us all along. We respond to The One who continuously invites us to become fully alive in Him. Our identity of origin — made in the image of God — finds rebirth as we connect with God in this intimate way. ***In our honest admission to God and learning how to relate to Him as Father, we are becoming the most blessed of all people.***

Only now, however, is the evangelical church beginning to realize that without spiritual direction, without one-on-one or small group conversations where our lives are laid open in the presence of a person gifted to discern the workings of our inner life, the disease of deception will not be cured. Without spiritual direction, millions of Christians will continue to walk

the "OLD WAY," thinking they're on the path to knowing God well.
Larry Crabb, *The Pressure's Off pg 42*

A New Sheriff in Town

When we face the true facts about ourselves, we are equipped to confront the self-deception that has hurt us and others. Admitting to ourselves the exact nature of our wrongs disarms the deceived and idolatrous parts of us which have dominated our lives. In effect we tell ourselves, "The game is over; there is a new sheriff in town." It's a revolutionary change within. Personally, I've had to be very direct with myself in order to turn my allegiance away from my addictions and toward God. My admission to myself was both a personal surrender and a claim of personal defiance to that faker-impostor part of me.

I give each of you this warning: Be honest in your estimate of yourselves, measuring your value by how much faith God has given you.
Romans 12:3 *NLT*

If we claim that we're free of sin, we're only fooling ourselves. A claim like that is errant nonsense. On the other hand, if we admit our sins – make a clean break of them – he won't let us down, he'll be true to himself. He'll forgive our sins and purge us of all our wrongdoing. If we claim that we've never sinned, we out-and-out contradict God – make a liar out of him. A claim like that only shows off our ignorance.
I John 1:8-9 *MSG*

Recovery requires that we accept ourselves and admit that which is the worst about us, and when we do this, there is a discovery of grace as only God can give. Grace is only grace when it's unwarranted. ***In grace we find permission to surrender the outcome of a war that is impossible to win. The war is over, we surrendered our illusions and ourselves and survived our addictions and lived.***

I quit focusing on the handicap and began to appreciate the gift.
It was a case of Christ's strength moving in on my weakness.
Now I take my limitations in stride, and with good cheer, these
limitations that cut me down to size – abuse, accidents,
opposition and bad breaks. I just let Christ take over! And so
the weaker I get, the stronger I become.
2 Corinthians 12: 7-10 *MSG*

The heart is the deepest essence of a person. It symbolizes
what's at our core. The heart of the matter is that we can know
and be known only through revealing what's in our heart.
Brennan Manning, *Posers, Fakers & Wannabes pg 147*

One of the great returns on the investment my honesty brings to me is when others in our fellowship say *"me too"* to me. When someone says *"me too,"* they are in effect telling me that *"they too"* have suffered from similar conflicts, shortcomings and sins as I have. In doing so, they help heal my perspective and how I relate to other people.

A timely "me too" helps deliver us from the power of our secrets. Identifying and admitting shared destructive patterns breaks down the walls of isolation. ***The experience of being heard, observed, known, included, loved and embraced, in spite of our addictions, sins and mistakes, is transformational.*** When a person gives the power of love through an understanding ear, compassion and understanding soak in deeply, washing away the poison of self-hatred and condemnation. ***Without the establishment and re-establishment of trust with other people in this way, spiritual and emotional wholeness cannot happen.***

Personal admissions of weakness and failure to another person may seem like a surgery of the soul, but doing so results in the freedom of a new way of thinking about ourselves, God and other people. To not risk honesty, to not trust, to not heal, to not become relationally and emotionally whole, leaves us alone and at the mercy of sexual addiction, inevitably leading to more failure and destruction.

When we lose the foundation of trusted relationship, we have no one to trust but ourselves, and yet it is the self that feels most foolish and incapable of making safe and solid decisions. We are in a trap. We are cut off from others. We hate our desire. We want relief from our pain. We want someone to care and comfort us, but we also want justice, vengeance. The dark desire to make our betrayer pay places us in a strange position of being both a victim and an abuser.

Dan Allender, *The Healing Path*

"What comes into our minds when we think about God is the most important thing about us."
A.W. Tozer

NEXT STEPS

You might be wondering at this point, "Who is the person I'm going to get real with and make my admissions to? Where do I find them?" Here, I will share with you the suggestions I followed and was glad I did.

Pick someone of the same gender, perhaps from your list of "higher powers." A local pastor or clergyman often works well, but not always. A competent counselor or medical professional can be very helpful in matters related to recovery from addiction. Above all, seek a person you believe to be trustworthy, someone who is able and committed to keep your confidentiality. I was fortunate to find someone who exemplified the love and acceptance of Jesus. I suggest you do the same because ***your listener will become your advocate in recovery just like Jesus is your advocate with God. Look for someone who expresses confidence in your ability to recover based on the power of a loving God.*** Someone who has suffered from their own addictions and is recovering is most always a good choice. You want a person who is capable of looking past whatever self-deception that is still inside of you, one who can intuitively see your truest self, seeing you as God sees you — someone who will not ignore personal dishonesty, but who will be understanding and patient with you. Look for someone who can and who is willing to offer you advice, someone whose advice you would follow.

Once you find the person you are going to get real with, share with them what you are intent on doing and why you feel they have something to offer you. It is imperative that you let them know you have become addicted sexually and you know you need help from others to recover. Respectfully ask them for their time, explaining that it may take more than one appointment. (These conversations can't be rushed if they are to be effective.) Share with them your desire to develop a growing faith in God and more honest relationships with other people, and pledge to them your commitment to be as honest as you can be.

I suggest you share with them what you have thought about yourself, others and God. But leave the faults of others out of the discussion. The wrongs of others are not your most pressing concern right now and obsessing on them may deepen your resentment and anger. ***Stick with the facts about yourself, avoiding unnecessary drama, exaggeration and minimization.***

"Tell the truth. It will confound your
enemies and astound your friends."
Mark Twain

Once I spoke honestly with another person about my life and my addictions, I found it helped to take some time for personal reflection. So, I spent time alone and I thanked God for the courage and opportunity I had experienced. I realized God had been there in the midst of conversation I had with this other person. I was reminded once again that ***God is always there when I show up honestly, with the truth about myself. He is always one step ahead of me.*** I also wrote down what I experienced, and I shared it with others in my recovering fellowship.

Having had this "first of its kind" personal experience, I enjoyed an amazing time of sitting, quietly and peacefully experiencing my body, my mind and my heart at peace and at rest with one another. The angst, the personal resentment, and the distrust I had felt since childhood was gone. And in its place was a feeling that the world we all live in is a good world and I was a good part of it. I thanked God for the experience. I asked Him to help me continue to grow in honesty, and give me strength to consistently surrender the bondage I had lived in for so long. I felt that my experience of living with other people had been changed, and I had been changed too. ***I knew my recovery was not complete and that I still was very capable of addictive self-destruction, but I also knew I was no longer alone, and I did not have to bear the burden of my faults alone, but they were shared.*** I felt alive in a large way, part of a world of imperfect and wonderful people, who when honest with God and others, will know the strength and capability of giving life amidst all hardship and sorrow. Sharing is caring. We become a living miracle in the lives of others when we share.

Personal Reflections

Viewpoints of change

CHAPTER SIX

We became entirely ready to have God remove all these defects of character.

—Step Six from the Twelve Steps

Humble yourselves before the Lord and He will lift you up.

—James 4:10

I'll never forget the trouble, the utter lostness, the taste of ashes, the poison I've swallowed. I remember it all — oh, how well I remember — the feeling of hitting the bottom. But there's one other thing I remember, and remembering, I keep a grip on hope: God's loyal love couldn't have run out, his merciful love couldn't have dried up.

—Lamentations 3:19-22 *MSG*

Just think how much more the blood of Christ will purify our hearts from deeds that lead to death so that we can worship the living God. For by the power of the eternal Spirit, Christ offered himself to God as a perfect sacrifice for our sins.

—Hebrews 9:14 *NLT*

DISCOVERING NEW DESIRE

I consider myself more fortunate than most for having had so many addictions. My addictions have enabled me to enjoy a perspective many people cannot see. The complex and multi-faceted nature of my drunkenness, drug use, and the generally pathetic way I lived my life proved to me beyond any doubt that I was in need of a complete personal overhaul. It also had become clear to me that the way my addictions to *things* changed back and forth confirmed that *things* like alcohol, drugs, or sex were not my most core problem. ***My biggest problem had been me; namely the way I thought about myself, about my life, and about God and others***.

With this reality coming into focus, I could see that for as far back as I could remember, I was deeply unhappy and dissatisfied with who I was and the life I lived. My best intentions and heartbreaking failures fused together over the years until I was entirely ready to be made into a fundamentally different kind of person. And I must confess I was also deeply concerned I might soon die because of my addictions if I did not change. Staying the same was no longer acceptable. I wanted to be different. I needed to be different.

DISSATISFACTION AND DESIRE – GIFTS FROM GOD

Dissatisfaction and desire are gifts from God. They are unique human qualities that reveal much of what is in our heart. For an addict, dissatisfaction with himself can be a gift from God because it can create the profound desire to change. Dissatisfaction and the desire it brings motivate us to take action; they are required if we want to recover from sexual addiction.

Blessed are those who hunger and thirst for righteousness…
Matthew 5:6 *NLT*

The dissatisfaction I felt within motivated me to do whatever I could do to stop living out my addictions. No longer could I be satisfied to just sit in the center of my problems alone, looking up and hoping or expecting things would change. I knew I had to change, too. I was ready for things to change in my heart, my mind, and in my character. I wholeheartedly wanted to escape my addicted life and become the kind of person who could live life well — someone who would make valuable contributions to the lives of others.

Until we become discontent with the rigors of trying to escape our powerlessness we will live locked into the present status quo. If we are fully at home in our situation, then we will not ponder a better tomorrow. Discontent is the mother of invention. Discontent is holy when it compels us to dream of redemption.
Dr. Dan Allender, *The Healing Path pg 84*

The real desire for real change grows up and out from the soiled reality of our corrupted life when it is examined and compared side-by-side with something better. If we are not dissatisfied with our "status quo," our hope for change is only a pipe dream — a fantasy — a merry-go-round of addictive make-believe. Dissatisfaction is a good and authentic emotion. It ignites a desire for a better future, not only recovering from sexual addiction, but as people who are truly free in every way. ***We don't just want to be healed, we want our entire sexually addicted personality and character reformatted and changed by the perfect design of God.***

> No matter what we do or where we hide, we can't escape our essential design. We long to be free of shame's restraints, immersed in the passion of giving and receiving. We long to live a sacrificial life that matters today and tomorrow.
> Dr. Dan Allender, *The Healing Path pg 107*

BALANCE AND RESPONSIBILITY

One challenge we face in long-term recovery is to balance our needs for love, personal security, and social position. As addicted self-centered people, our beliefs and values regarding our personal needs have probably been distorted. We have often ignored our needs or denied them. And other times we expected others to meet our needs because we were too lazy or self-centered to be responsible for ourselves. We thought we knew what we needed, and we expected someone else to do for us what only we could truly do for ourselves. Or, on the other hand, we would think no one would be there to help us, so we wouldn't honestly communicate our needs and feelings, which further compounded the isolation and helplessness we felt. Either way, the self-preoccupation we felt increased, hardening even more the self-centeredness that caused our problems. ***Self-centeredness is the root cause of all our character defects and sins.*** It can be called self-idolatry, and it is deadly to a sexual addict — and everyone else as well for that matter. But however, as we remain diligent in our recovery work, this is changing. Our self-centeredness begins to die off and fall away when we reach out to God and others honestly and openly. And in doing so we learn not to make such quick assumptions regarding what is best for us or for others either. Our first thought can often get us into trouble, so it is important that we make good second thoughts — praying and consulting with others in order to make the best decisions possible, which results in the best actions in just about any situation. ***Just because our head sits on our shoulders does not mean it is our friend.***

Since most of us are born with an abundance of natural desires, it isn't strange that we often let these far exceed their intended purpose. When they drive us blindly, or we willfully demand that they supply us with more satisfactions or pleasures that are possible or due us, that is the point at which we depart from the degree of perfection that God wishes for us here on earth. That is the measure of our character defects or if you wish, of our sins.

Alcoholics Anonymous, *12 Steps and 12 Traditions pg 65*

Misguided feelings of personal inferiority or superiority, grandiose and unrealistic beliefs, selfish intentions, selfish motives and selfish priorities are all symptoms of a deeper problem. If we believe that our demands must be met or if we believe it's somehow bad to feel pain or have difficulty, or if we believe that others need to make us happy, we are exposing ourselves as the selfish center of our lives. Recovery in Christ will give you ever-increasing opportunities to make good choices leading to an abundant life. But! ***There is always one absolutely wrong choice! And that is to make yourself the center of your own world.*** God has never shared His role with anyone, and He won't share it with any of us. Our character defects and sins thrive when we try to rule our own lives or anyone else's.

Our character flaws ooze out of us like a foul odor when we remain stuck, living life our way. On the other hand, as we focus our mind and our heart on God, we become more willing to let go of our character defects, our addictions and the habitual sinfulness that has held us back in our lives. It is important to note that even ***when we express our trust in God in the***

smallest ways, it shows we are growing in willingness. This growth in willingness is a growth in faith, and no matter how small our willingness and faith is, it pleases God. Willingness is our part in our growth. We plant it like a seed — no one can do this for us, we do it for ourselves — our recovery fellowship and partners will help us nurture and grow our seedlings of positive change. Our brothers and sisters in recovery who help us tend our new garden of change — and we theirs — are in effect a huge down pouring of God's caring rain. Seedlings of willingness and faith respond dramatically as we make these small and crucial choices.

"Faith as small as a mustard seed."
Matthew 17:20

EMOTIONAL TRIGGERS

While doing my Step Four personal inventory work, I started to see how the difficult emotions I experienced could be powerful triggers for my addictions. As emotions are triggers, character defects are the building blocks of addiction, and self-centeredness is the cement which holds the addicted nature together within me. So, finding the freedom to recover and live in a way that was healthy long-term was impossible without removing these addicted structural components from me.

I know today how my character defects started innocently when I was a child. They were my means of survival. I learned to manipulate to get my needs met. I lied to protect myself. I hid my emotions to avoid embarrassment and shame. I rationalized to escape ugly truths which were too much for me to handle. My character defects were really nothing more than broken and ineffective tools I used for coping and control. They were my methods of minimizing pain, and diffusing perceived threats. They were my strategy to care for myself when I believed that no one else would. At times I feared what life would be like for me without my character defects. When I felt that a character defect — like my lying — was necessary to survive, I would mourn the thought of having it removed from me. Fortunately, my sponsor and counselor and recovery partners helped me see how fearing the loss of one of my coping mechanisms was understandable, but it was also critically important for me to grieve these personal losses without complaint so I could move on down the path of my recovery.

I knew I had made the decision to turn my will and my life over to the care of God daily and, as I did this, the self-centered cement holding my addictions together began to slowly erode. There was little I could do to avoid the difficult emotions I felt. They came and went like the wind. All I could do was recognize them and speak honestly about them to a trusted recovery partner or spiritual guide. ***And while I could make the decision cognitively to get rid of the addicted building blocks of my character defects, my best efforts seemed to actually reinforce them. So, like everything else in my life, I turned them over to God, asking Him to remove them in a way that fit His plan for my life. Then I began doing whatever I could to live without them in the future***.

THE GIFT OF GRATITUDE

During this time of my recovery I began to experience a deep untangling of the pressure and stress I had felt inside me. I was learning new and healthier ways to cope without taking drugs, drinking alcohol, or being sexual in ways that made me feel bad about myself. I was trading in my troubling and self-destructive emotions for the simple gift of gratitude, often without even knowing I was doing it.

Gratitude posts a loving guard at the door of our lives, insuring that bitterness and resentment and anger will no longer dominate us as they have in the past. Gratitude helps us to be thankful for life as it is not how we wish it, expect it or even need it to be.

If you will throw away your detestable idols and go astray no more, and if you swear by my name alone, and begin to live good lives and uphold justice, then you will be a blessing to the

nations of the world, and all people will come and praise my name.
Jeremiah 4:1 *MSG*

As gratitude inside of us increased over time, it became more apparent that we had to continue taking effective actions to avoid a relapse back into active addiction. We needed to be ever alert, because sexual addictions interact with, set off and build upon other addictions. The dual diagnosis of addictions is becoming more and more common in rehab centers and Twelve Step fellowships. So with this in mind, we stay closely connected to other recovering people who have more experience than we do. We look to our sponsors, our mentors and our counselors for help and guidance. They help keep us moving away from our addictions, or unknowingly picking up new addictions along the way. Common co-addictions can be food and compulsive eating disorders, destructive spending, gambling, alcohol and other drug addictions and even prescription medications. Religion and religiosity can be addictive, and we can become so obsessed with certain people that we become addicted to trying to control them or their life. Fact is, not recognizing any destructive behavioral pattern can potentially trigger sexual addiction. This is because, ***at their core, addictions are simply a destructive relationship with a mind or mood altering substance or experience that expresses***

itself in destructive behavior. Virtually anything that is mood or mind altering and destructive can potentially be addictive.

If you think you may have a problem with a substance, even the use of prescription or 'legitimate' drugs, it is essential that you stop and get help today. If you are drinking destructively, seek professional help and call Alcoholics Anonymous at once. And the same holds true for any addictive behavior. You and your loved ones will suffer more if you don't ask for the appropriate help today.

Today and every day we stand at a crossroad. But, we are not alone. When we are ready to ask for help, a fellowship will be with us. Even better, THE SOURCE of all power has already joined the battle for our lives, helping us live a new way and become new people, to be free.

Your God is present among you, a strong warrior there to save you. Happy to have you back, he'll calm you with his love and delight you with his songs. The accumulated sorrows of your exile will dissipate. I, your God, will get rid of them for you. You've carried those burdens long enough.
Zephaniah 3:17, 18 *MSG*

Becoming Aware

One suggestion I found helpful was to refer back to my personal inventory and review the journaling I produced after I admitted the exact nature of my wrongs to another man. When doing this, my journaling showed me how my beliefs resulted in patterns of actions and reactions. The more I understood these patterns, the more my character defects appeared in bold print. These questions helped me:

- Have I had difficulty admitting to others my need for help?
  Pride

- Have I been in debt or preferred my desires over someone else's?
  Greed

- Have I gotten mad because someone else was more privileged than me?
  Envy

- Have I lived out my life in a fearful way?
  Trusting more in myself than God

- Have I compared my insides with the outward appearance of others?
  Self-objectification

- Have I looked at outside appearances, ignoring the feelings of others?
  Lust & Objectification

- Have I felt compelled to please others more than God?
  Approval seeking

- Have I been frustrated when others have not lived as I wanted them to?
  Codependency

- Have I feared to be alone?
  Emotional dependence on others

- Have I or my family suffered from my work schedule?

  Being a workaholic

- Have I felt the need to keep certain facts about myself secret?

  Dishonesty

- Have I had habits of unhealthy eating?

  Personal self-abuse

- Have I procrastinated doing things I know should be done?

  Laziness

- Have I believed my life would change without me changing?

  Fanciful Thinking

Facing our character flaws in this manner shows we are seeing ourselves in a more honest way. Appreciate the deeper level of personal self-honesty you are capable of. You are heading in a good direction!

NEVER FORGETTING

As we progress in our recovery, it is easy to feel as if we are "recovered," which can result in us becoming complacent and blind to the insidious nature of sexual addiction. Perhaps your spouse has returned to you, your boss is happy with your work again, and your bills are getting paid on time. These are all good things of course, but to keep recovering from your addictions, you must not lose sight that there is still more work to be done.

There are more questions to be asked and more answers to be revealed.

Monitoring ourselves thoroughly and recognizing our character defects honestly and consistently provides life-giving insight for our lives. How have our character defects impacted the lives of others? Have our selfish actions ever turned out well for us or for anyone else? Do we display kindness and goodness to others sincerely, or is our kindness just an act that hides our selfish desires? Forgetting important lessons we have learned along the way is catastrophic.

Good friend, don't forget all I've taught you, take heart my commands. They'll help you live a long, long time, a long life lived full and well.
Proverbs 3:1, 2 *MSG*

To admit discontent and hunger for redemption requires that we face our part in the problem and compels us to yearn and dream of more.
Dr. Dan Allender, *The Healing Path pg 85*

Do you think about how God is working in your life? Do you ponder the progress you're making, the fellowship you have discovered and the better life that you have today? These are all gifts from God who, even before you ever first admitted your need for help, has been working to bring you the help He knew you needed.

Keep a remembrance journal, or carry a small notebook to record your thoughts. Share your thoughts — good or bad — with those who support you in your recovery work. The journal notes you make will be an exciting real time history of the growth of your new life. And this will enable you to see the work of God to be amazingly, miraculously more than anything you could ever have done on your own. Thanksgiving and gratitude will become even more alive in you, further strengthening you for your continuing journey to healing and wholeness. The best is yet to come!!

I am filled with awe by the amazing things you have done. In this time of our deep need, begin again to help us, as you did in years gone by. Show us your power to save us.
Habakkuk 3:1, 2 *NLT*

REVERSING THE PAST

We know it is not possible for us to fix all our character defects on our own, but we can reverse the actions that reinforce our character defects. ***Letting go of character defects is never passive. Change within a man is a divine interaction between God's grace and our choices. Like everything else we do in recovery, character change requires action.*** Changing our actions helps to interrupt habitual patterns of thinking, believing and feeling. MOTION CHANGES EMOTION!

When we realize that we are reacting with a character defect, addicted feeling or thought, we can choose to do the opposite of what our addicted instincts were inclined to do. If the old way of thinking, feeling and acting didn't work in the past, we know from experience it won't work now. So we try something different.

While we cannot change the past, we are never doomed to do the same thing time after time in the future. We can choose to do something different, avoiding the painful and destructive results that came from our addicted life. It will take some practice, but with a little commitment and a few failures along the way — which we shared with another person — the changes to thinking, feeling and acting can actually come quite quickly. Those of us who came from religious backgrounds will call this repentance, and that is exactly what it is. Grassroots, down and dirty, rubber meets the road, repentance. The simplest definition of repentance is to "change one's mind." It is an about-face. It is turning and going in the other way. Whatever you call it, it works.

And so I insist – and God backs me up on this – that there be no going along with the crowd, the empty-headed, mindless crowd. They've refused for so long to deal with God that they've lost touch not only with God but with reality itself. They can't think straight anymore. Feeling no pain, they let themselves go in sexual obsession, addicted to every sort of perversion. But that's no life for you! You learned Christ! My assumption is that you have paid careful attention to him, been well instructed in the truth precisely as we have it in Jesus. Since then, we do not have the excuse of ignorance, everything – and I do mean everything – connected with that old way of life has to go. It's rotten through and through. Get rid of it! And then take on an entirely new way of life – a God-fashioned life, a life renewed from the inside and working itself into your conduct as God accurately reproduces his character in you.

Ephesians 4:19-23 *MSG*

PERSONAL REFLECTIONS

PERSONAL REFLECTIONS

Asking for directions

Chapter Seven

We humbly asked Him to remove our shortcomings.

—Step Seven from the Twelve Steps

Don't copy the behavior and customs of this world, but let God transform you into a new person by changing the way you think. Then you will know what God wants you to do, and you will know how good and pleasing and perfect his will is.

—Romans 12:2 NLT

And we can be confident that he will listen to us whenever we ask him for anything in line with his will. And if we know he is listening when we make our requests, we can be sure that he will give us what we ask for.

—I John 5:14-15 *NLT*

You can be sure that God will take care of everything you need, his generosity exceeding even yours in the glory that pours from Jesus.

—Philippians 4:19 *MSG*

A Newer You

There was a lot I needed to learn to keep moving away from my addictions. Fortunately, I had come to know a number of people who were successfully living their own addiction recovery process. They generously shared their experience with me, which was a great help.

One of the important things they shared with me was to ***think of the word humility or "humbly" as an attitude that chooses to follow God's will over my own will.*** This appeared to be very simple. But doing it has been difficult, and I have not always made it happen like I would have liked. Making this decision consistently marks a deep shift at the core of my character, who I am, and the way I live my life.

Now today, when I do think "humbly," it feels like I live in a place where impossibly good things happen to otherwise impossible people like me. I experience peacefulness, even when the world as I know it gets turned upside down, inside out, with things changing all around me. *Humility helps me feel like my life is becoming right.* Like life makes sense. On the other hand, when I choose to go my own way, which I often do without even realizing it, my self-abusive tendencies return, I struggle with self-preoccupation and the silly notion that my life revolves around me. *When I try to be the master of my own kingdom, humiliation becomes almost inevitable.*

Learning the true meaning of humility was new to me because as a child I learned a distorted meaning of humility from my family. I was taught to confuse humility with self-loathing and self-hatred. From their example of abusing themselves and one another, I learned that it was "humble" not to like myself. By grade school, I believed my feelings of uselessness, self-pity and defeatism meant that I was "humble." This was not my family's intention, but their confusion about humility resulted in confused and angry family relationships.

Real humility has nothing to do with a low self-esteem or a negative self-image. Low self-esteem is often the result of not understanding the care and concern God has expressed for us in His Word. Misconceptions of God create spiritual and emotional blindness and this can cause us to betray ourselves without knowing it. *Self-betraying thinking triggers self-betraying behavior, which is hand in glove with our addictions.* And, with denial being a stronghold of addiction, we become all the more blind. We rationalize. We make excuses. *Our low self-esteem becomes a sick excuse to stay stuck in our miserable condition.* It becomes a sad and sick way of saying, "I don't want to be responsible. I don't want to be held responsible."

Recovery is impossible as long as we find excuses — or reasons —not to change, even when our excuses and reasons are rooted in our family of origin or the way we were raised. Blaming others does not work either. By blaming others for where we are today, we try to put the problems we are responsible for on to others who most certainly should not accept them. We are the only ones who can take real responsibility for our lives. And this requires — yes — humility.

> For just so long as we were convinced that we could live exclusively by our own individual strength and intelligence, for just that long was a working faith in a Higher Power impossible. This was true even when we believed God existed. We could actually have earnest religious beliefs which remained barren because we were still trying to play God ourselves. As long as we placed self-reliance first, a genuine reliance upon a Higher Power was out of the question. That basic ingredient of all humility, a desire to seek and do God's will was missing.
> Alcoholics Anonymous, *12 Steps and 12 Traditions pg 72*

FACING THE FACTS

My first encounter with real humility came when I recognized and admitted my addictions. And I grew in humility as I worked to see myself more honestly when doing my personal inventory. The work I did made it possible for me to humbly 'own' the facts about myself. When I have the real facts about my choices and my life, and see them realistically with clarity, I am less inclined to rationalize my destructive actions, minimize my difficulties or ignore the pain others have suffered because of my character defects. When I know the facts of my life, I know my own limitations and can accept my own needs and shortcomings.

You and I, as humans, are not all-powerful. We do not control ourselves all of the time, nor do we control other people any of the time. Humility helps us to see these facts, giving us the eyes through which we will see God change who we are, the way we think, the way we handle our emotions and the way we act. As we are changed on the inside, our lives change on the outside.

So, I have learned to think of my improving character development as a responsibility and a gift at the same time. The growth and maturity I experience is a gift God gives to me as I responsibly admit and correct my character defects in the most honest way I can. When I notice my character defects expressed in my thoughts and actions, I choose to change my thinking and my actions as well. My character defects lose some of their power when I do this. Every time I say no to them, the grip they've habitually had on me loosens a bit. Nothing is so helpful to healing addictions and changing character defects than to stop doing the addiction and change the way we live our lives day-to-day. ***Great empowerment comes from God when we live in obedience.***

As we work and make progress in our recovery, our priorities and the things that concern us will become re-oriented. We will discover a humility that desires obedience more than blessing and character growth more than comfort — all so that we may help and not hinder the work of God. ***The greatest blessing for any sex addict is to live free from addiction, fully aligned with the will of a loving God.*** Even before we asked, we received from God everything we ever needed. He satisfies our heart! ***God is always one step ahead of us!***

Humble yourselves under the mighty hand of God, that He may
exalt you in due time, casting all your care upon Him,
for He cares for you.
I Peter 5:6-7 *NLT*

A great turning point in our lives came when we sought for
humility as something we really wanted, rather than as
something we must have. It marked the time when we could
commence to see the full implication of Step Seven.
Alcoholics Anonymous, *12 Steps and 12 Traditions pg 75*

I can't count how many times — usually motivated by guilt and religiosity — I would ask God for patience, only to get angry with myself if patience didn't show up when I wanted it to. This obviously proved I wasn't really interested in being more patient. I think what I really wanted was to feel relief from the tension and other uncomfortable feelings I was experiencing at the time. With what I now know, *I find it much more helpful to me to simply admit to God and to someone else the fact that that I struggle with being an impatient person.* I tell them, sincerely, I want to change, to think, and to act differently, in a more patient way, as I move forward in life. Seeing myself honestly and sharing what I see is humility for me. This builds a willingness to ask others for direction and a humility with which to follow the direction I receive.

Saying, "Dear God, I want to be more patient" sounds good, but we may miss the subtle demand we are making, holding God responsible for our character defects and problems. But by saying "Dear God, I am an impatient person and I want to change," we offer up the truth about ourselves and we accept responsibility for being impatient. ***Humbly asking is asking for change internally, with no demand for changes to the current conditions or external circumstances. Changes in our circumstances are optional; changes in our character are necessary.*** We become the changes we desire. The ultimate purpose of all prayer is to get hold of God, and to do so, we let go of our pride, inviting God to act according to His purpose in our lives. God will be our strength. He will empower us to do what we are responsible to do.

My Creator, I am now willing that you should have all of me, good and bad. I pray that you now remove from me every single defect of character which stands in the way of my usefulness to you and my fellows. Grant me strength, as I go out from here, to do your bidding. Amen

7th Step Prayer, *The Big Book* of Alcoholics Anonymous

Character defects cultivate and facilitate our addictions. They reduce us to shame-filled, fearful little children. When we face and admit the failures we most want to hide from others, we discover God has been waiting for us patiently, ready to make a life-transforming connection with us. Moving to become His in this way, we get hold of a life and goodness that was impossible before. We let go of the personality characteristics which have held us back for so long, so nothing will keep us from *"knowing the measure and stature of Christ."* Though previously we were ruled by lusts, addictions, and other people, we are becoming the kind of people who admit our character defects and, in doing so, we more fully receive the transforming spirit of Christ. In humility, we become good and powerful men.

God's kingdom is like a treasure hidden in a field for years and then accidentally found by a trespasser. The finder is ecstatic – what a find! – and proceeds to sell everything he owns to raise money and buy that field.
Matthew 13:44 *MSG*

Our relationship with God and our spiritual growth must always come first, being more important than career, hobbies, church, even our friends and family. This is because without recovery, nothing else matters very much because nothing else will survive our addictions. Anything good stays good only as we couple our humble heart with God's love and care. Without Him, nothing is worth having.

> So in terms of what every man needs most crucially, all man's power is powerless because at its roots, of course, the deepest longing of the human soul is the longing for God, and this no man has the power to satisfy.
> Frederick Buechner, *The Magnificent Defeat pg 33*

THE SOURCE OF OUR STRENGTH

God did not create the problems we have with our character, but now we are asking Him to change the character problems that trouble us. We have been living by our own strength, trying to overcome things we could never overcome in our own power. As we surrender our lives to God, humbly asking Him to remove our shortcomings, we connect with His strength in a way unlike we have ever encountered before. Only in God and with the help of others can someone who has become sexually addicted receive the endurance, the stamina and the strength to consistently let go of their character defects and addictions. Just like everything else, we entrust our character and its defects to God. *And the timing God chooses to use in removing our character defects serves His purposes.* The best thing we can do is to accept the pain and difficulties we have caused as opportunities to learn and grow, so that we can benefit from these lessons once and for all.

As we work to grow away from our character defects, there will be many times when we fail, sometimes repeatedly. Inevitably we'll find ourselves in a place where we must choose between trusting God once more and applying our best efforts, even though all our previous attempts have ended in failure. Failure to try is in and of itself a failure to trust God. ***What we choose to do with failure is the profound indicator of who we are and who we will become.*** Failure with effort can be a frustrating setback, which produces sorrow and the discouraging feeling we will never overcome our lusts. Setbacks are inevitable so let's make peace with the reality of their existence. It is in the midst of our failures and setbacks where we find the humble opportunity to keep turning to God to be the Source of our strength.

For God can use sorrow in our lives to help us turn away from sin and seek salvation. We will never regret that kind of sorrow. But sorrow without repentance is the kind that results in death.
2 Corinthians 7:10 *NLT*

We can accept God's good gifts too easily. Grace can be accepted only when we face our own inabilities. Forgiveness can be embraced only when we lay bare our wrongdoing, and hope can be imparted only when we face the reality of our own despair.
Charles Ringma

ARE YOU WILLING?

Being unwilling to let go of a character defect or addiction is dangerous, potentially sabotaging our entire recovery effort. Unwillingness certainly limits our growth. When I felt like I was holding onto a character defect I didn't want to let go of, I admitted my doubts, the fear I felt, and the stubbornness I felt inside. I admitted all these to myself, to God, and to another person. I also prayed and asked for God to help me with the fear and pride I was experiencing. I asked that He help me let go of everything that stood between me and a closer relationship with Him. The discovery of grace has never relieved me of my responsibility for taking the appropriate actions to deal with my character defects. When I'm in doubt about my attitude or character, I ask my sponsor or someone else who knows about my addictions and my desire to recover.

The moment we say, "No, never!" our minds close against the grace of God. Delay is dangerous, and rebellion may be fatal. This is the exact point at which we abandon limited objectives, and move toward God's will for us.
Alcoholics Anonymous *12 Steps and 12 Traditions pg 69*

If we still cling to something we will not let go,
we ask God to help us be willing.
Alcoholics Anonymous, *The Big Book pg 76*

Letting go of character defects starts with acting as if God has already equipped us — and He has — to live well without them. We take the opposite action we would have taken if we were acting out with a character defect. We reverse course, acting as if God has given us what we need, and in religious terms, we repent. If I want to be like Jesus, admitting my struggle and failure, then acting in faith like I am becoming like Jesus is a great place to start. ***Over time, honest obedient actions begin to change the way we think. If you want your life to change, change the way you act.***

It is obvious what kind of life develops out of trying to get your own way all the time: repetitive, loveless, cheap sex; a stinking accumulation of mental and emotional garbage; frenzied and joyless grabs for happiness; trinket gods; magic-show religion; paranoid loneliness; cutthroat competition; all consuming-yet-never-satisfied wants; a brutal temper; an impotence to love or be loved; divided homes and lives; small-minded and lopsided pursuits; the vicious habit of depersonalizing everyone into a rival; uncontrolled and uncontrollable addictions, ugly parodies of community. I could go on. This isn't the first time I have warned you, you know. If you use your freedom this way, you will not inherit God's kingdom. But what happens when we live God's way? He brings gifts into our lives, much the same way that fruit appears in an orchard – things like affection for others, exuberance for life, serenity. We develop a willingness to stick with things, a sense of compassion in the heart, and a conviction that a basic holiness permeates things and people. We find ourselves involved in loyal commitments, not needing to force our way in life, able to marshal and direct our energies wisely.
Galatians 5:19-23 *MSG*

PERSONAL REFLECTIONS

Caring for others along the way

CHAPTER EIGHT

We made a list of all persons we had harmed, and became willing to make amends to them all.

—Step Eight from the Twelve Steps

Do to others as you would have them do to you.

—Luke 6:31 *NLT*

And why worry about a speck in your friend's eye when you have a log in your own? How can you think of saying, `Let me help you get rid of that speck in your eye,' when you can't see past the log in your own eye? Hypocrite! First get rid of the log from your own eye; then perhaps you will see well enough to deal with the speck in your friend's eye.

—Matthew 7:3-5 *NLT*

For if you forgive men when they sin against you, your heavenly Father will also forgive you. But if you do not forgive men their sins, your Father will not forgive your sins.

—Matthew 6:14-15 *NIV*

Seeing the World Around Us

Everything we say and do affects the lives of those around us in one way or another. Maybe big, maybe small, and maybe not even realized today, but our actions do solicit response, reaction and consequence — and not only for us, but for the whole world, beginning with those closest to us. Like it or not, good or bad, we impact this world.

My sponsor and counselor drove this point home to me — the reality of my social and relational responsibilities. With their help, I could better see the hurtful impact my life had on others. I came face-to-face with my shortcomings which grew out from my self-centeredness. I had lived my life for myself, and other people had suffered because of it.

Now in recovery, I am more honestly aware of my shortcomings. They illuminate my need for God, getting me in touch with my frustrated desire to experience life in a way only He can give me. I am seeing myself and the world differently. Even though life can be difficult, I view it with enthusiasm. I like this new life. It is a better life than I have ever known before. But as good as I feel, there remains a deep, nagging sense that I have unfinished business. Also, my counselors, sponsors, and mentors urge me to be cautious and thoughtful. They remind me over and over again that "my new life in

Christ" will be short-lived if I forget or ignore how I have negatively impacted the lives of others.

DON'T WASTE YOUR RECOVERY

We waste our recovery efforts when we forget our failures. Forgetting failure is a form of delusional self-centeredness. Forgetting separates us from the responsibility of our failures, as if they never happened, or they no longer exist, when in reality they do. ***When we forget our failures, when we compare ourselves favorably with the faults of others, when we look to find imaginary non-existent success for ourselves, or when we trade an honest spiritual relationship with God for cheap religious pretending, the most insidious kind of self-centeredness develops — self-righteousness.*** When we avoid the reality of how we have hurt others, we become piously religious, self-absorbed and self-satisfied, disconnected from the difficult world we have created for those around us and for ourselves. We create inside ourselves the exact Pharisee we so enjoy condemning in others.

An essential part of recovery is to recognize and admit personal responsibility in relationships. We must be willing to acknowledge and admit to ourselves and to at least one other person how other people have been hurt by our selfish attitudes and actions. Recovery requires that we seek forgiveness, honestly. It demands we help those hurt by the way we have lived our lives. This part of our recovery work makes it possible for us to reconcile with others. And regardless of whether or not others are willing to reconcile with us, we are always responsible to forgive others. We must forgive so we can grow in our recovery.

So, we recognize our selfishness and resentments the best we can. If we can't do this fully, we admit it. We admit our doubts and shortcomings of faith and intention to God *and* another person. Then, we begin investing in the lives of others, working to help heal the world around us one person, one situation at a time. Doing this consistently builds a positive momentum that changes the way we view ourselves, and the way we relate with others. We then expand this momentum of growth and change to our families, our communities, our workplaces and our churches. God will build a new personality in us. We will become more mindful of loving others, honoring them as people who are created for the purpose of knowing God and His love. Today, it's not just ourselves and our circumstances that we want to see changed and improved. We want to see other people healed and their circumstances improved as well.

Becoming Relationally Response-Able

The power to love and live well is a gift from God. It's the joyous gift of living well spiritually and relationally. As we become more spiritually connected with God and as we develop healthier relationships with others, we become healthier people ourselves. As we become responsible to others for our actions, we will become response-able with our wives, our children and our vocations. Our individual place in the world will begin to make sense. We will find our place in this world to be a very, very, very good place.

With all of this in mind, our job at this time is to make a list of the people we have hurt and become willing to forgive others for any wrongs they have done to us. *Doing this helps us become ready to make things right.* There are no excuses. No ifs, no ands, and no buts. Excuses, procrastination and delay may be understandable, but they are unacceptable if we intend to grow in recovery. ***Excuses stop recovery dead in its tracks.*** The calling of Christ in recovery is to make our list and become ready to make things right wherever we can. There is no good reason we should not do this. There is no good reason to delay.

"Therefore, if you are offering your gift at the altar and there remember that your brother has something against you, leave your gift there in front of the altar. First go and be reconciled to your brother; then come and offer your gift."
Matthew 5:23-24 *NIV*

The Poison of Resentment

During the process of making my list, I got in touch with resentment I felt for some people who hurt me deeply in childhood. I asked for God's help to forgive them, but it was difficult. I also asked for help with this from my sponsor and my counselor. With their help, I was able to begin admitting my resentment, communicating honestly why I felt the way I did. This helped me be responsible — response-able once again — for my own feelings which in turn helped me be more forgiving to myself and others.

Today I recognize that, while others have accidentally and sometimes even intentionally harmed me, ***any resentment I hold against others becomes a root source of my own spiritual and emotional handicaps and pain.***

Resentment poisons our hearts. Then it circulates into every part of our lives. It's like taking poison and expecting someone else to get sick and die.

Variation of original quote from Malachy McCourt

As I learned to quit looking for opportunities to be resentful and blame others, I became more objective about myself and my life — better able to embrace my shortcomings and my strengths. I could sense ***God's strength moving into me through my weaknesses, resulting in a more intuitive ability to care for others without fear.*** And, I learned to better care for myself as a child of God. Benefiting from the forgiveness others may give to us starts with us forgiving others.

> Don't speak evil against each other, my dear brothers and sisters. If you criticize each other and condemn each other, then you are criticizing and condemning God's law. But you are not a judge who can decide whether the law is right or wrong. Your job is to obey. God alone, who made the law, can rightly judge among us. He alone has the power to save or destroy. So what right do you have to condemn your neighbor?
> James 4:11-12 *NLT*

This work will help us sense the incredible work of God in our lives. We will see how He has made us for supernatural purposes — with His divine purposes in mind. As we list those we have hurt, and as we become willing to help them, we start to pass along some of the goodness God has given to us in recovery. ***Our personality, our talent and our charm will never be enough. People need a love that is not based on who we are. They need a love based on the One whom we all have been created for.*** Attempts to love made by our own power, no matter how dedicated, most often take on the ugly ways of codependency. ***Loving others effectively grows from an obedient connection with Real Love, and this comes only from — you guessed it — God.***

New Discoveries

I realized some amazing things as I made a list of the people harmed by my addictions. I came to grips with how amazing it was that I was ever loved by anyone, considering the selfish ways I treated other people. I saw that — when I came face-to-face honestly with the truth of my addictions — I wasn't loved because I deserved it, but because God and others saw me from a perspective of love. This made me value my relationships like a precious gift. Now, with every ounce of diligent response-ability I can muster, I view others lovingly, as others have done for me.

Caring for others respectfully in this way — with love-centered actions — I will hope that love will be given back to me, but I won't need to be upset if it's not. My truest God-given desire is to just pass along the love I receive from God and others. So, moving through any fear of rejection I may feel, I live my life differently than I had in the past. I care for others as I would like them to care for me — just as God, my sponsor and counselor have done for me.

"Until you conquer the fear of being an outsider,
an outsider you will remain."
C.S. Lewis, *The Weight of Glory pg 154*

We set realistic boundaries for ourselves, and we accepted boundaries others placed on us. First, we became willing to make amends to others. ***Real hope for reconciliation requires that we be willing to make our amends unconditionally.*** Second, we became willing to accept healthy limitations and to make living amends by the way we relate to others in the future. There is little value in professing good intentions. ***There is much greater value when we live our lives in healthy socially responsible ways, letting the authenticity of our changing life speak for us.*** If we refuse the opportunity to right a wrong, we shut the doors and windows of the spiritual home God is building within us. Nothing gets in, nothing gets out. Darkness closes in and we miss the leading of God's Spirit. We simply create more of the chaos that we are trying to avoid.

It's quite easy to agree intellectually with the facts of our wrongdoing, to look past our mistakes and not be responsive to the hurt others feel because of us. Intellectualizing our lives disconnects us from feeling our emotions. It blocks our ability to connect with others. It reduces our amends to little more than a narcissistic continuation of the selfishness we claim we want to be free of. ***A recovering man, however, moves from his head to his heart and from his heart to his feet, where reconciliation with others is made step-by-step.*** With our feet placed firmly on God and within a fellowship of support and accountability, we find stability to live response-ably. As we are willing to accept responsibility for our life, good and bad, we are better able to know ourselves like God knows us. ***As we're willing to know and own ourselves, both good and bad, we will live in reality, the place where God lives.***

By the time I was an adult, my resentments had rooted so deeply that I was no longer consciously aware I felt the way I did. My anger had become internalized, fueling the fires of my addictions. One day in a counseling session my counselor had me read something written by someone in their early recovery. By the time I read the third sentence I broke in tears, and it took me several minutes to compose myself. Waiting patiently, the counselor asked me what I was feeling. The only response I could give her was that I had been waiting all of my life for the freedom these words expressed. Later that day I went home and wrote the following.

"I survived childhood physical, emotional and sexual abuse. But now, I no longer consider myself a victim. With God's help, a change has come over me — my attitude is different. No longer do I need to destroy myself or others with anger and hate. I don't need to entertain thoughts of revenge. God knows what happened. He knows all the facts. He knows the truth. He will make the correct judgments and punishments as He sees fit and according to His mercy. He will be just. I leave it in His hands.

I will not be judged for what happened to me, but I will be judged by how I let it affect my life and how my life affects others. I am responsible for my actions, for what I do with what I know. I am not to blame for what happened to me as a child. I cannot change the past, but as God is my strength, I can change my future and I can assist others with their future. I have chosen to be healed and to take full advantage of the opportunities to be healed. As I heal, I choose to pass this healing onto my children, my family and to others. The ripples of healing in the pond of my life will spread throughout future generations."

Personal Reflections

Personal Reflections

Honoring others along the way

CHAPTER NINE

We made direct amends to such people wherever possible, except when to do so would injure them or others.

—Step Nine from the Twelve Steps

This is how I want you to conduct yourself in these matters. If you enter your place of worship and, about to make an offering, you suddenly remember a grudge a friend has against you, abandon your offering, leave immediately, go to this friend and make things right. Then and only then, come back and work things out with God.

—Matthew 5:24 *MSG*

We love each other as a result of his loving us first. If someone says, "I love God," but hates a Christian brother or sister, that person is a liar; for if we don't love people we can see, how can we love God, whom we have not seen? And God himself has commanded that we must love not only him but our Christian brothers and sisters, too.

—1 John 4:19-21 *NLT*

I tell you, love your enemies. Help and give without expecting a return. You'll never — I promise — regret it. Live out this God-created identity the way our Father lives toward us, generously and graciously, even when we're at our worst. Our Father is kind; you be kind.

—Luke 6:35-36 *NLT*

EMBRACING THE WORLD AROUND ME

My sponsor consistently spoke to me about my social and relational responsibilities, which meant working to repair the damage and hurt my addicted life had caused other people. It has always been and always will be our responsibility to initiate peace and healing in relationships. With this in mind, I began the work of helping others recover from pain I caused them, pain they did not ever deserve. And, my sponsor also told me, the best way for me to continue my own recovery work was to help others, especially those who have been hurt by me and my addictions.

Making amends is not easy. Any recovering sex addict will tell you that making amends is very challenging work. It can be complicated too, because we may face situations where we need to make amends to people who deeply resent us. As much as we would like to have one, there is no magic wand in recovery or in making amends. If we go looking for a magic wand, we will lose ourselves to a world of fantasy and make-believe. Recovery only happens in the real world. If we really want to recover, we will be willing to live in the real world. Making amends is not optional.

God blesses those who work for peace, for they will be called the children of God.
Matthew 5:9 *NLT*

FACING FEELINGS

Many of us have held deep anger and resentment against certain people who were hurt by the actions of our addicted life. For years, I resented a person who could have stopped the abuse I suffered as a child. For reasons I may never know, this person chose to do nothing when he could have protected me — a small child. The anger I felt for him was so deep I did not even realize I felt the way I did. I repressed my rage as I grew older, and my addictions increased along with my rage. I became rude and thoughtless toward others, including, of course, the person who ignored my needs. My rage blinded me, making it impossible for me to see how I had hurt this person and others close to him. Even though this person and I lived in separate parts of the country, my addictions and selfishness brought pain and hurt into his life, as well as my own.

I can no longer side-step my feelings. I had to confront the feelings of anger I felt against this person, so, with help from others, I did. Even though the wrongs this person did to me far exceeded what I had done to him, I could no longer hold his wrongs against him if I was going to heal from my addictions. So I got in touch with him. I apologized to him for my actions, and offered to do whatever I could do to repair the hurt I had caused him. As heartbreaking as it is, today many years later, this person has never acknowledged the abandonment and pain he caused me, and I sadly suspect he never will. Nevertheless, his refusal to acknowledge his lack of care for me as a young child is none of my business today. *I forgive him today and every day, not because he is innocent or because he deserves forgiveness. I forgive him so that I can recover and move on from the damage he did to me.*

Occasionally, the anger and resentment I felt for this person come back. But today I diligently work to let go of any remaining resentment I feel. While I have no real relationship with this person, today my attitude toward him, myself, and my family history has radically improved. I am much more honest about how things were for me growing up. I no longer make excuses for my family or for myself. Things simply were the way they were and they are the way they are. My hope is that someday things may change between this person and myself, that we can have a healthy family relationship. I also hope this person will one day see that my life and values are worth appreciating. However, moving forward and trusting God's plan for my life, I remind myself that this person's attitude toward me is none of my business. It is between him and God. I can hope for forgiveness but I am never entitled to it.

TRUE FORGIVENESS

True forgiveness can only be given and received; it cannot be earned or demanded. ***True forgiveness does not condone, excuse or minimize wrongdoing. True forgiveness looks directly at the wrong and wrongdoer, knowing full well the impact of the wrongdoer's actions, recognizes them for who and what they are, and offers the offender the mercy and grace of a restored, but changed relationship.*** Both giving and receiving forgiveness is an act of humility. People who really forgive look upon others, even the most disturbing, and see them as someone whom God loves and cares for. People who forgive honor God by honoring all people with esteem, respect and love, no matter how undeserving they may be.

This does not mean that all our relationships with others will be as they were before. In all likelihood, our relationships with others, while hopefully reconciled, will be changed forever due to boundaries, which other people will require as we move back into relationship with them. We may never again experience the freedom with them we had before. We may never enjoy certain relationships as we have enjoyed them in the past. We may never again have the unmitigated trust of our families. Others, for understandable reasons, will set boundaries on us. It is important we recognize these limits are a direct result of the pain and hurt we have caused. We are responsible for our pain and for making things right wherever we can. We should accept these limitations respectfully. We respect the lives of others in the same way we hope to be respected in the future.

It is not until we love a person in all his ugliness that we can make him beautiful, or ourselves either.
Frederick Buechner, *The Magnificent Defeat pg 42*

At times, I struggled to forgive those who had hurt me, so I prayed for them. I found ***praying for them helped me*** to move beyond the resentments that blocked my growth and recovery. I prayed God would give them hope for their life, help for their difficulties, grace for their struggles, and courage to live abundantly. I prayed for them in the same way I prayed for myself. As I prayed for others in this way, I realized that any entitlement I felt about others forgiving me made any forgiveness I receive meaningless. Entitlement reduces forgiveness to foul, codependent, shallow and graceless appeasement. And I am sure you will agree with me that this is not what we want. Feeling appeased will not help us recover. We need to recover from our addiction, and helping others heal from the damage we caused is our responsibility — regardless of any damage, others may have done to us. Period!

Now you can have sincere love for each other as brothers and sisters because you were cleansed from your sins when you accepted the truth of the Good News. So see to it that you really do love each other intensely with all your hearts.
I Peter 1:22 *MSG*

Put yourself aside, and help others get ahead. Don't be obsessed with getting your own advantage. Forget yourselves long enough to lend a helping hand.
Philippians 2:3 *MSG*

And just as others may place boundaries for us, we may need to establish boundaries for others. When others have done inexcusable things to us, we need to recognize these things for the inexcusable things they are. We should discuss them with our sponsor and our counselor. Their guidance will give us needed insight to make important decisions about what kind of relationships we want and what kind of boundaries need to be in place so our relationships will be safe and sane and healthy going forward.

We need not ever excuse inexcusable acts that people may do, but we do need to forgive people because forgiveness is essential for life. This is essential for both offender and victim to have a healthier and happier life ahead. For our part, we must be careful not to ask God or others for "forgiveness" when we are really asking to be excused for our wrongdoing. ***Wrongdoing is not an accident. Accidents can be excused, but selfish people who do selfish things need forgiveness.***

Sincerely asking for forgiveness is an act of repentance. And repentance does not debate, it does not bargain, and it never rationalizes or makes excuses. When confronted about our wrongdoing, we never dispute the facts. We let the charges and criticisms be what they are. Asking for forgiveness has nothing to do with making excuses. It is a simple brokenhearted request for undeserved mercy.

ACTIONS SPEAK LOUDER THAN WORDS

In making my amends, I made every effort to speak thoughtfully to those I had hurt. I put them above myself, and tried to speak wholeheartedly with respect and reverence. Where I had shown disregard and selfishness before, I now tried to reflect the image of God's love. I considered it my job — my response-ability once again — to give back to them the dignity I had stolen from them. I acknowledged to them that they never deserved to be treated the way I treated them, that they in fact deserved much better. I expressed my desire to make things right between us, starting with a change in my attitude toward them, reflected in the way I would interact with them in the future. The message I had for them was very simple: Today I see things different than I did in the past. I am less important; God and other people are more important.

There were times when I felt other people were out to get me somehow. Sometimes they were and sometimes they were not. However, whether people were or were not out to get me was not the important issue. This is because when I was willing to see what God had for me to learn in any situation, I found most of the attacks I felt were directed at my addictive thinking, my selfish actions and my sinfully distorted way of relating to others. So today, I do my best not to defend myself when I feel attacked. When I have done something wrong, triggering an aggressive response from someone else, I simply apologize for what I have done wrong and ask them what I can do to make things right. Then, above all else, I change my attitudes and my actions. Yes, you have heard it before — actions speak louder than words.

This is the kind of life you've been invited into, the kind of life Christ lived. He suffered everything that came his way so you would know that it could be done, and also know how to do it, step by step. He never did one thing wrong, not once said anything amiss. They called him every name in the book and he said nothing back.
I Peter 2:21–23 *MSG*

The people who gave you the consequences are not your enemies. By seeing those who give you consequences as the enemy, you keep yourself stuck in justifying your behavior. Your real problem is your denial and self-delusion.
Patrick Carnes PhD, *Facing the Shadow pg 16*

Many of us in Operation Integrity felt quite nervous about making amends to other people. One thing we learned in the process was that making amends to ourselves helped create spiritual and emotional momentum and this helped us move forward and make amends to others. This is because building healthier relationships requires that we address the many ways we have hurt ourselves. ***While some may dispute this, no one has suffered more from sexual addiction than the one who is sexually addicted.***

Many of us needed to make changes in our eating and exercise habits — or lack thereof. When we had hurt ourselves financially, we faced it and with the help of our sponsors and counselors, we made changes to develop financial integrity. When we had hurt ourselves emotionally through self-pity and by blaming others, we faced it and discussed it honestly with others. Sometimes we even wrote ourselves amends letters, addressing them to ourselves at specific ages from our childhood and life. Sitting privately in front of a mirror, we read these letters to ourselves, face-to-face. We also read these letters to our sponsors, and to our counselors and select recovery partners. We gave ourselves grace and understanding. And we made peace with our ups and downs. ***Recovery is never a straight line from beginning to end. No matter how good or how bad things get, one thing is for sure; things are going to change.***

EXPERIENCING THE FREE LIFE

Making amends plays an important part in helping us learn to love ourselves freely in a similar way that God loves us. This freedom to love ourselves is more than just a freedom from addictions; it is a freedom to experience life in a spiritually empowered way. For example, we will no doubt experience fear at times, but living in a spiritually empowered way will enable us to live courageously even in the face of fear. We will feel pain, but we will be able to express kindness to others and even ourselves regardless of the pain we feel. We do not 'possess' this freedom, but it never really leaves us either. This freedom is a by-product of knowing God's forgiveness personally; being assured that He will never take His forgiveness from us. Yes, we can ignore and even turn our backs on Him and His live-saving and empowering forgiveness, but it will never be out of reach when we are *sincerely* ready to receive it. There are days where we can stop, look back, and see how far we have come by the grace of God. These are days worth living for.

It is not possible to love others unless our hearts are growing in faith and hope. Faith and hope birth love as we live out our calling in anticipation of his coming.
Dr. Dan Allender, *The Healing Path pg164*

Because of the way sexual addiction creates problems for our relationships, we consulted with our sponsors and counselors about the most appropriate way to speak with our loved ones in hopes of making amends to them. It was important that we speak to them honestly about our addiction without hurting them by sharing unnecessary or salacious details. Sharing the facts in a general way opens the door for communication. And it opens the door for others to honestly share their feelings with us. Without causing others additional pain, and without airing our dirty laundry to the whole world, we bring caring and thoughtful communication into the broken relationships we created. With respectful and discreet honesty, it becomes possible to make things right and possibly rebuild broken and damaged relationships.

In situations where we faced serious consequences or the possibility of strong temptations, we once again asked our sponsors and counselors for guidance. Some amends should not be made face-to-face. Other amends may have to be postponed for a better time. We will be of little benefit to anyone if, in our attempts to clear our own conscience, we make ourselves sacrificial lambs or march needlessly into overwhelming temptation. Our sponsors and counselors helped us to know how to handle each situation. They helped us to see that there is rarely a good reason to hurry. It is far better to make amends well than fast!

A Word of Caution

We should use great caution before contacting any sexual partners we used in our addiction. Old partners, with no ill will, can easily derail our recovery. We must stay safe from any situation where we can possibly lose the freedom we have gained. If God wants us to see former lovers, He will arrange it in a way where we can be safe.

And while it may not be wise to contact old partners directly, we can begin to make amends to them by assisting people who essentially represent them in some way. For example, changing our attitude toward women in general and giving all women dignified respect is a great beginning. ***Letting go of our memories of sexual conquest and our fantasies is a great place to start in making amends to former partners.*** When no longer seeing women as objects for amusement and pleasure, and by redirecting our minds by praying for those held hostage in our memories and fantasies, the power our memories and fantasies have had on us in the past will begin to lose its grip. When we face a provocative situation, or remember an exciting experience from the past, we pray for the people we have held captive in these fantasies and memories. We pray for their health, their safety, and for their happiness. We pray they would experience the fulfillment of their most sincere hopes and dreams. When doing this consistently, we developed healthier ways to deal with troubling thoughts and memories and with the spontaneous stimulations that once drove us to do things we would later regret. ***By making amends to specific women, and by making amends to those whom we will never or cannot ever see again, we partner with God in retraining our instincts and this allows us to view women more humanly — and interact with them in a new more wholesome way.***

When we acknowledge the God-given beauty inside of all women, we see past the delightful and sometimes overwhelming distraction of a woman's beautiful body, seeing her as God sees her. Women are not only beautiful, they are free, independent and autonomous creatures, created to live free from the sexualized pressure we unknowingly create when we only see them for their sexual attractiveness. We do not need to "have" women. We can enjoy them as friends.

Personal Reflections

Staying alert on the way

CHAPTER TEN

We continued to take personal inventory and when we were wrong, promptly admitted it.

—Step Ten from the Twelve Steps

You could easily fall flat on your face as easily as anyone else. Forget about self–confidence; it's useless. Cultivate God–confidence.

—I Corinthians 10:12 *MSG*

How can I know all the sins lurking in my heart? Cleanse me from these hidden faults.

—Psalms 19:12 *NLT*

We justify our actions by appearances; GOD examines our motives.

Proverbs 21:2 *MSG*

INTEGRITY

Many of us — and I include myself in this — can be overly concerned with how we appear to others. This can get us trapped into living in ways that are inconsistent with how we truly want to live. We can find ourselves more concerned with looking good in the eyes of others, than being good no matter who is watching us. Integrity is impossible without interpersonal authenticity. Reputation without character is an illusion. ***We have to get real with ourselves and with others, no matter what others may think or say about us, if we want to recover.***

The hidden realities of our innermost thoughts and feelings manifest themselves in the way we live. Continued movement away from our addictions requires that we be aware of our motives and the innermost thoughts and feelings behind them. We must surrender our counterfeit self-perceptions and appearances to God, honestly express who we really are, which means preferring His plan for our life more than our own — in every way. Moving forward requires that we never forget that we are powerless over our sexual addictions and that our lives are beyond our ability to manage on our own. In addition, let us never forget that when life seemed most hopeless, we saw how other people were recovering from their addiction and —

because of the miracle God was doing in their lives — we came to believe we could recover from our addictions too. We then made the decision to trust God with our lives the best we knew how, recognizing that our relationship with Him must always grow as He directs. We accepted the opportunity for recovery as a gift and a responsibility. In other words, we worked to obtain a more honest understanding of ourselves and our failures.

We began admitting to ourselves, to God and to well-chosen people who and what we really were inside and out. Sharing ourselves with others honestly, we found ourselves becoming more and more dissatisfied with the pathetic way we had masqueraded through life. We knew we needed God's help to change our character defects, and we asked Him for it. Over time, our character defects weakened and our eyes opened, which made us more aware of how we had hurt people around us. We now do our best to reconcile with others, starting with forgiving anyone who has hurt us, and helping anyone who has been hurt by our addictions. This simple recovery plan has been taking us, step-by-step, on a journey where we have begun to see a new character, and a new life within us. But we won't stop now. We can't stop now. What benefit would we have, what usefulness could we offer to others, if we abandoned our recovery journey incomplete?

I don't mean to say that I have already achieved these things or that I have already reached perfection! But I keep working toward that day when I will finally be all that Christ Jesus saved me for and wants me to be. No, dear brothers and sisters, I am still not all I should be, but I am focusing all my energies on this one thing. Forgetting the past and looking forward to what lies ahead, I strain to reach the end of the race and receive the prize for which God, through Christ Jesus, is calling us up to heaven.
Philippians 3:12-14 *NLT*

PRACTICE MAKES PROGRESS

I practice these recovery principles every day. Seeking to have an honest view of myself and monitoring my own motives, helps insure my progress in recovery. God does not tell me to bring my failures to Him once. He tells me I should bring my failures to Him continuously, day in and day out.

So let's not allow ourselves to get fatigued doing good. At the right time we will harvest a good crop if we don't give up, or quit. Right now, therefore, every time we get the chance, let us work for the benefit of all, starting with the people closest to us in the community of faith.
Galatians 6:9 *MSG*

God is in charge of human life, watching and examining us from the inside and out.
Proverbs 20:27 *MSG*

Recovery is a continuously ongoing process of character development. I cannot be what I am not. However, with practice, I can make progress. When I lack character, I admit it. When admitting my lack of character, I make myself available — honestly — to character improvement. Improvement in my character comes to me more like a gift from God than something I have earned on my own. Every time I admit my wrongdoing and sincerely rededicate myself to correcting my mistakes the best I can, I live more deeply within the framework of God's character, which helps me to think, react and live more effectively in the future. To quit pretending takes practice and good practice makes good progress.

If the Spirit of God detects anything in you that is wrong, He does not ask you to put it right; He asks you to accept the light, and He will put it right. A child of the light confesses instantly and stands bared before God; a child of the darkness says – "Oh, I can explain that away." When once the light breaks and the conviction of wrong comes, be a child of the light, and confess, and God will deal with what is wrong; if you vindicate yourself, you prove yourself to be a child of the darkness.
Oswald Chambers *My Utmost for His Highest March 23*

What helps at this point is to see your consequences as your teachers. You have been sent a lesson to learn. If you don't learn the lesson this time, it will manifest itself again, and probably in a more painful form the next time.
Patrick Carnes Ph.D. *Facing the Shadow pg 17*

Recovery is an everyday kind of work. Daily, I do my best to guard myself against pride, arrogance and over-confidence. Nothing gets wasted when I do my recovery honestly. My failures even provide great motivation for change and growth. As we get into the habit of honestly sharing ourselves with others, we become the men we want to be: real men.

On my bad days, I tend to think about my failures. On my good days, I tend to think about my successes. But! On my best days, I tend not to think about myself at all. This is because I am too busy thinking about God and others.

The power to honor the truth – to speak it and be it – is at the heart of true masculinity.
Leanne Payne, *Crisis in Masculinity pg 41*

PERSONAL REFLECTIONS

Nourishment and rest

CHAPTER ELEVEN

Sought through prayer and meditation to improve our conscious contact with God as we understood Him, praying only for the knowledge of His will for us and the power to carry that out.

—Step Eleven from the Twelve Steps

Let petitions and praises shape your worries into prayers, letting God know your concerns. Before you know it, a sense of God's wholeness, everything coming together for good, will come and settle down. It's wonderful what happens when Christ displaces worry at the center of your life.

—Philippians 4:6, 7 *MSG*

Here's what I want you to do: Find a quiet, secluded place so you won't be tempted to role-play before God. Just be there as simply and honestly as you can manage. The focus will shift from you to God, and you will begin to sense his grace.

—Matthew 6:6 *MSG*

Be still in the presence of the LORD, and wait patiently for him to act. Don't worry about evil people who prosper or fret about their wicked schemes.

—Psalm 37:7 *NLT*

LISTEN INTENTLY SPEAK SOFTLY LIVE POWERFULLY

I have never had a better life than the one I have today. I had hoped for a life like this growing up. As a child, I saw my friends attain functional abilities that escaped me until recently. So much of my life was lost in self-loathing, envying others, and feeling isolated, wondering what was wrong with me. Thankfully, things have changed. Today I am thankful to be alive. Joy has overwhelmed me as the result of accepting God's grace and giving myself to Him. But, as full as I feel now, I also still feel restlessness within me. Called from Eternity, I yearn relentlessly for something deeper — something more. It is as if I have walked a thousand miles excited to get home, but the last mile is a steep uphill climb home. This is nothing new for me, really. Much of my life was spent chasing earthly pleasures like social prestige and financial security in an attempt to satisfy my soul. It is clear to me now, that I am created with a desire for more, and I am not alone in this desire. ***The undercurrent of every destructive behavior is a yearning that exists unheard and unsatisfied, because no earthly thing will satisfy anyone.***

Every man or woman who has come to our fellowship has, by their own admission, failed to satisfy the deepest longings of their soul. No matter how hard we tried, our efforts to satisfy our deepest longing was only temporary, always failing to satisfy our innermost selves. ***We surrendered our lives to God, not because we were good or honorable or even because we wanted to at the time; we surrendered our lives to save them! No one gets God by personal virtue. He is discovered only when a bankrupt man or woman honestly seeks Him.***

Every one of us has our own personal reasons for surrendering our lives to God, and some sound very good, while others sound pathetically selfish. And this is okay because there is never a bad reason to ask God for his help. Any and every reason we have to recover from the broken condition of our lives is a good one. However, over time we learn to seek God for reasons that are more honest. ***We learned, and are still learning, to surrender for the best reason — God Himself. We came to Him because we had to; we stayed with Him because we learned to live in grace.*** There is no better place for a recovering man or woman to live.

Soul Yearnings

While the yearnings of my soul have never disappeared, they have changed. In a deep and personal way, I am evermore aware of a relentless longing in my soul that is not fully satisfied, yet fulfilled when directed toward God in Christ. I am completed as I honor God as the Giver of Life, the Sustainer of Life, the One who by His nature is Life.

Recovery requires that we simplify our lives beginning with recognizing what is most core about us — our God-created spirituality. This spirituality — simplicity — can only be experienced when we live the life God offers us everyday. It is as simple as this: with God, life has infinite possibilities for good; without God, real goodness in life is impossible. Remembering this simple principle will transform everything we think, feel and do, molding us into the kind of people who live in private the same way we would if all eyes were on us.

We must be motivated from within, not from without. We must live our lives before God, knowing that He sees all and that our reward will come from Him if we persist in doing what He has asked us to do.
Joyce Meyer

Our sponsors, spiritual directors and counselors have been and will continue to be important resources for us in recovery. They were my helpers in growth, but, while I have relied on them in many ways, they are not my resource or power for recovery and change. What they offered was good, but I need something more. As a "*new man in Christ*" identity grows in me, I take on a personal identity that is much more from the influence of God working deep within me than the good character qualities other people help me learn. I am learning not to confuse a teacher with *The Teacher*. Human teachers come and go, but God will never leave us or forsake us. I am His. We are His. He is ours for Eternity.

NO ACCIDENTS IN RECOVERY

We suffer when we get stingy with surrender. The bigger our ego gets the smaller God gets. However, when we look to experience God's presence in our life, our ego shrinks correspondingly. Only after, and never without, the intentional application of hard work, will we grow up. We remain humanly imperfect in this growth process, but internally we become complete at the same time. We experience the purpose God made us for, a purpose our created nature requires, which is why there are no accidents in recovery.

One of the powerful miracles of recovery is the story that grows out of a person's experiences as their life transforms. As you and I live out our recovery and share it with others, our life story will encourage others just as we have been encouraged through the stories of other recovering people. Healthy balanced people who express their lives as living miracles show how God takes all the broken pieces of our lives and creates something worthwhile for all to see, proving there are no accidents in recovery.

If we have never had the experience of taking our casual, religious shoes off our casual religious feet – getting rid of all the excessive informality with which we approach God – it is questionable whether we have ever stood in His presence.
Oswald Chambers, *My Utmost for His Highest January 3*

We take our efforts seriously, while knowing that serious results are from God. We remain intent and dogged in pursuit of our disciplines, in the working of the steps, but dismiss at all times the notion that our work is enough. It never is. Our miracles come from God, and He offers them in conjunction with our work.
Oswald Chambers, *My Utmost for His Highest February 9*

Everything we have admitted expresses how alone we have been in the past. With the help of others in recovery, we have discovered and accepted our great need for God. We have been adulterous lovers who having been found out, come home awkward and embarrassed and ashamed — sneaking in the back door, not knowing what to say. Now — having been *'found out'* — we realize that God has already made the first move to build a new relationship with us. He listens to us as we become willing to make the second move, which is to pray. ***Prayer takes us out of our aloneness.***

This is what I think, in essence, prayer is. It is the breaking of silence. It is the need to be known and the need to know. Prayer is the sound made by our deepest aloneness.

Prayer is man's impulse to open up his life at its deepest level. People pray because they cannot help it. In one way or another, I think, all people pray.
Frederick Buechner, *The Magnificent Defeat pgs 126 & 126*

I believe every one of us is inclined to pray, we all do it in one way or another. We intuitively need and want to engage something bigger than we are. In whatever way we do it, prayer is our way of saying hello to God. Prayer puts us at the kitchen table, with coffee in hand, ready for a meeting, a dialogue, an increased closeness of relationship. Prayer ushers us into communion with the Perfect Father. And while He, Our Father – God, is perfect, our prayers do not need to be perfect. What we do not know how to say, He says for us. What we find impossible to express, He understands. Prayer catapults us into the frontier of an authentic spiritual life.

In prayer, real prayer, we begin to think God's thoughts after Him: to desire the things He desires, to love the things He loves, to will the things He wills. Progressively, we are taught to see things from His point of view.
Richard J. Foster, *Celebration of Discipline pg 34*

Instead of all these, the answer that He gives, I think is Himself. If we go to Him for anything else, He may send us away empty or He may not. But if we go to Him for Himself, I believe that we go away always with this deepest of all our hungers filled.
Frederick Buechner, *The Magnificent Defeat pg 127*

Prayer is always the most relevant thing I do. To be free from my addictions, my compulsions and my self-centeredness, I must become a man who prays. Prayer helps me find a link between the catastrophe of my past and the God-designed providence of my future. Prayer helps me know exactly who I am and what I should do at any moment in time. In prayer, I find the alertness to live well in any difficult moment and the energy to meet overwhelming challenges. Prayer helps me work with God to build my future, to determine what kind of man I will be, and what kind of impact I will have on the world. Sometimes, it is helpful to pray for others to change. Most importantly, it is always helpful to pray for me to change. As I am changing through prayer, prayer changes the influence I have on my surroundings. Then, through the lens of this new *prayer-full* perspective, I see the world around me change.

> Keep on asking, and you will be given what you ask for. Keep on looking and you will find. Keep on knocking and the door will be opened. For everyone who asks, receives. Everyone who seeks, finds. And the door is opened to everyone who knocks.
> Matthew 7:7-8 *NLT*

A DIFFERENT KIND OF WORK

All relationships are a two-way street, which include conversations and mutual disclosures. Prayer — conversation with God — is no different. Meditation is our listening part in our conversation with God. It is the way we hear His voice, discern His directions, and accept the power we must have to obey His instructions. Recovery requires a significant amount of hard work, but meditation is a different kind of work. Meditation is not about effort; it is about quieting our mind, body and spirit so we can hear what we need to know. Often times the best thing we can do for our own spiritual life is to stop. Stop working. Stop playing. Stop everything. Be still. Be quiet. Listen.

In contemporary society our Adversary majors in three things: noise, hurry, and crowds. If he (the enemy) can keep us engaged in "muchness" and "manyness", he will rest satisfied.
Richard J. Foster, *Celebration of Discipline pg 15*

Hurry is not of the Devil, it is the Devil.
Carl Jung

In meditation, we set distractions aside the best we can. We take time in our lives for God. We intentionally create time, place and space for Him and we listen for His presence in the space we set aside for Him. When doing this, we can see how He works to reorganize our concerns and priorities in ways, which are healthy and useful. Our agendas and motivations become re-worked supernaturally. God does not speak to any of us because of our special abilities. He speaks to every one of us when we are honest before Him, when we are open to obey Him and want to hear from Him.

We learn to meditate by doing it — by meditating. We learn how to do it much like we learn how to do anything else. We start, get distracted, start again, get distracted and then start again. Over time, and with every renewed start, we will be more capable of listening, hearing and discerning the voice and will of God. We lose nothing in this process because real meditation does not empty us or detach us from that which is truly important. Meditation actually results in a filling and re-attachment of our heart and mind to God's heart and mind. It helps us gain a deepening friendship with Jesus. Meditation will build an expectation in us for God to speak to us personally, that He will act on our behalf beneficially, and He will teach and guide us to courageous action. God will ensure that we will always understand His guidance when we really want to know it.

Because most of us have never really done it, mediation may feel intimidating and uncomfortable. It sure was for me. Nevertheless, we best not put pressure on ourselves. ***We do not have to meditate well; we just have to do it***. Part of meditation is allowing our imagination to run freely, like a child's does. God created us with imagination for a purpose after all. Our addictions deadened our capacity for creative thinking, but meditation re-opens us to the wonderful world of imagination, possibilities and goal setting that God has built into us. Thinking, imagining, and believing the many wonderful ways that God may reveal Himself to us, change us, restore us and use us, is important. Remember this though, God has no obligation to serve us, or fulfill any ideas we think up. Yes, He has committed Himself to care for us, but He is not obligated to give us all we think we should have. We must be careful not to allow meditation to become a breeding ground for selfishness and self-centeredness, which are most dangerous when they take on a religious tone. Guard against this kind of personal self-deception. If we are serious about walking with God, we must prefer obedience over comfort and blessing.

Are you seeking great things for yourself? Don't do it! But don't be discouraged!
Jeremiah 45:5 *NLT*

And yet the reason you don't have what you want is that you don't ask God for it. And even when you do ask, you don't get it because your motive is wrong – you want only what will give you pleasure.
James 4:3 *NLT*

Scripture is the grounding rod of all meditation. Our commitment to absorb Scripture helps keep our prayer and meditation centered and properly aligned with God's will for our life. Through the disciplines of prayer and meditation, we learn to listen intently, speak softly, and live powerfully.

We take our efforts seriously, while knowing that serious results are from God. We remain intent and dogged in pursuit of our disciplines, in the working of the steps, but dismiss at all times the notion that our work is enough. It never is. Our miracles come from God, and He offers them in conjunction with our work.

Oswald Chambers, *My Utmost for His Highest February 9*

Personal Reflections

Arriving, building, and inviting others

CHAPTER TWELVE

Having had a spiritual awakening as the result of these Steps, we tried to carry the message to others, and to practice these principles in all our affairs.

—Step Twelve from the Twelve Steps

Live creatively, friends. If someone falls into sin, forgivingly restore him, saving your critical comments for yourself. You might be needing forgiveness before the day's out. Stoop down and reach out to those who are oppressed. Share their burdens, and so complete Christ's law. If you think you are too good for that, you are badly deceived.

—Galatians 6:1-3 *MSG*

Then he turned to the host. "The next time you put on a dinner, don't just invite your friends and family and rich neighbors, the kind of people who will return the favor. Invite some people who never get invited out, the misfits from the wrong side of the tracks. You'll be--and experience--a blessing. They won't be able to return the favor, but the favor will be returned — oh, how it will be returned! — at the resurrection of God's people."

—Luke 14:12-14 *MSG*

Embracing what God does for you is the best thing you can do for him. Don't become so well-adjusted to your culture that you fit into it without even thinking. Instead, fix your attention on God. You'll be changed from the inside out. Readily recognize what he wants from you, and quickly respond to it. Unlike the culture around you, always dragging you down to its level of immaturity, God brings the best out of you, develops well-formed maturity in you.

—Romans 12:1-2 *MSG*

Destiny Arrives and We Show Up

I never wanted to be a sex addict. I never asked for it, and I certainly never intended it to take hold of my life the way it did. In fact, getting addicted to anything was the furthest thing from my mind. But when I realized how serious my problem was, all I wanted then was to recover from my addictions, because I was afraid I might die. However, through the ongoing process of my recovery, I have received so much more than I ever wanted or thought I might receive. The healing of my addictions has been, and continues to be, an incredible journey leading me into a radical kind of personal transformation. I have changed and I continue to change, gaining wisdom and insight that I could never get from a book, in a classroom or from another person.

I once thought of myself as a physical being trying to have spiritual experiences, but now I think of myself as a spiritual being that lives out physical experiences in ways God designed for me to live. As a man who has been sexually addicted, and having offered myself to God, I have become the most blessed of all men.

A New Purpose

As my recovery continues, gratitude for my addictions grows. I have learned to think of my addictions as preparation. I call them pre-recovery preparation. ***They have helped me become the kind of man who embodies the progressive prodigal experience of selfishness, disaster, desperation, hopeless cries for help, discovery of God's gracious power to change, and a life resurrected.*** There was no better plan for me. Now today, having used up every resource of my own, I recognize my purpose in life is to seek, discover and experience God as Jesus Christ knows God, and as I receive the benefits of knowing God, I encourage others to seek, discover and experience God for themselves. ***We are all prodigals in one way or another, after all.***

Listen to your life. See it for the fathomless mystery that it is. In the boredom and pain of it no less than in the excitement and gladness: touch, taste, smell your way to the holy and hidden heart of it because in the last analysis all moments are key moments, and life itself is grace.
Frederick Buechner, *Now & Then pg 87*

I am humbly proud of my growth and the growth of the other people who share their recovery with me. We are well prepared to do good business with God and with other people. God has a future for each of us that is uniquely designed for us by Him. When following His plan, we are well equipped to give goodness and love to whomever we encounter.

Now I still consider myself a sex addict. And I need to admit that my brain makes a spontaneous wrong turn every now and then, creating a conflict of impulse and desire inside me. ***Recovery has taught me that temptation is not a calamity.*** Temptation reminds me that I am a man at risk and that I must remain diligent in my recovery work and spiritual disciplines. The only thing insuring my recovery is the maintenance of my spiritual submission to God. He alone has the power to keep me safe and secure from my own selfish nature.

Sometimes, the feelings and temptations I experience are uncomfortable; other times, they are miserable. Nevertheless, no matter how conflicted I feel, I continue to admit that I am powerless over my addictions and that it is only through the life-changing power of Jesus Christ, that I will continue recovering from them. ***Each time I feel the urge to chase after my addicted — and attractive — way of life but do not, the impulses and compulsions that accompany these temptations lose some of their power.*** New attachments for goodness are established inside me with each obedient moment, ultimately gaining strength over the old disobedient ways. Moreover, I lose interest in my own life compared to the expanding joy of sharing God and His life with others. I prefer taking the personal spiritual revolution God has given me, and blessing the whole world with it.

Possessed by God

The gift of new life is not without a cost. I claim no ownership rights for this life God gives me — I am owned and possessed by God. Being aware of His grace gives me the gift of gratitude, which nourishes my new desires making every area of my life an act of surrender and worship. Through the grace of the Giver, I enjoy His gifts, and I become His as well. The gifts He gives to me are only mine to hold, to enjoy and to pass along.

For He claims all, because He is love and must bless. He cannot bless us unless He has us. When we try to keep within us an area that is our own, we try to keep an area of death. Therefore, in love, He claims all. There's no bargaining with Him.
C.S. Lewis, *The Weight of Glory pg 190*

This inrush of God's Holy Spirit heals us naturally – naturally. But it does far more than that. Indeed, as we pursue the spiritual life we lose sight of the physical benefits in our increasing vision of God Himself. We find after a while that we desire God more for His own sake than for ours.
Agnes Sanford, *The Healing Light pg 60*

"You can't keep it unless you give it away."
Alcoholics Anonymous

What started with Bill Wilson and Dr. Bob Smith, two alcoholics helping each other stay sober, has resulted in a movement that helps millions of people recover from alcoholism and drug addiction. AA has also spawned the Al-Anon movement, which helps millions of codependents and addicted families worldwide. Just like Bill Wilson and Dr. Smith, in recovery we become a gift to each other and to the world one moment, one situation, one person at a time. ***The greatest needs of our day will not be met by counselors, doctors and professionals. They will be met by recovering people like you and me.***

We are grateful leaders in pain suffered and humble leaders in recovery gained. We are men and women who have joined the fight for our own lives and for the lives of others as well. The great need in our world remains the same today as it has always been: godly men and women who display a quality of character and life that ignites a desire in others to know God in a way that changes them from the inside out. We have an important role to play and no one can live out this role better than we can. We call to anyone who is dead and dying in his or her struggles, problems, addictions and sins. We say to them, "Come with us, we are going to God. We are going to Life." Everyone needs what we have.

Those of us who are strong and able in the faith need to step in and lend a hand to those who falter, and not just do what is most convenient for us. Strength is for service, not status. Each one of us needs to look after the good of the people around us, asking ourselves, "How can I help?"
Romans 15:1 *MSG*

We want to live well, but our foremost efforts should be to help others live well.
I Corinthians 10:24 *MSG*

It's Not About Us

If we think our recovery and healing is ours alone, we have neither recovered nor been healed. When we believe our recovery and healing is to be lived to help others, we are recovering and healed already. There is only one choice to make and this choice never changes. We face it day in and day out, minute by minute, with every breath we take. Who owns us? Who will we live for? Will we live for God and others or die in addiction and shame? But, healing and serving others is not the end, it is just the start. All too easily, we compartmentalize our lives, gaining ground in some ways and losing ground in others, but it is our lives as a whole that really matters. ***We must be willing to give the whole of our lives to God the best we can or our life as a whole will not be His at all.***

Carrying a hope-filled message to people who suffer insures that we continue our growth in sexual integrity and recovery. It is impossible for us to live our lives in true service to God and others unless we are willing to die to our own addicted agendas every day, one day at a time. We must be willing to do what others have done for us, to turn our lives inside out where they can be useful to someone else. We must be willing to do all that we can do every day, one day at a time, to insure that we are cleansed and healed deeply, so someone else can come to us in their time of need and find answers to their questions and be guided into their own personal experience with Jesus Christ through us.

FINAL QUESTIONS

My recovery experience has changed the way I spend my time, my talents and my money, as well as changed the foods I eat and the way I conduct my career. Most of all, my recovery is best reflected in the positive changes in my relationships. I know my life is no longer my own. I have become, and I continue to become, the most blessed of all men. I am now much better able to share myself freely with others in rich, personal and even intimate soul-enriching ways. But there is still more personal recovery work for me to do. I continue moving forward, ready and willing to face tough questions so I may continue to recover and gain a fuller, more intimate relationship with God and the empowered life that only He can give.

Here are some of the questions I keep coming back to again and again…

What is God saying to me?

What is it that I am powerless over?

How is my life unmanageable?

What do I need to admit?

What am I going to do now?

What are the tough questions you need to ask yourself? Before, you and I avoided these kinds of questions as we hid out in the darkness of our addictions. We were afraid of the answers the questions might reveal. But now we know God gives us courage, which enables us to face difficult questions like these. We have learned they are a blessing because they keep us moving forward, leading us to a meaningful life that makes sense and is worth living well regardless of pain or suffering we may encounter. And after all, isn't that what we were looking for all along?

Personal Reflections

NOTES

Our
Journey Home
Insights and Inspirations for Christian Twelve Step Recovery

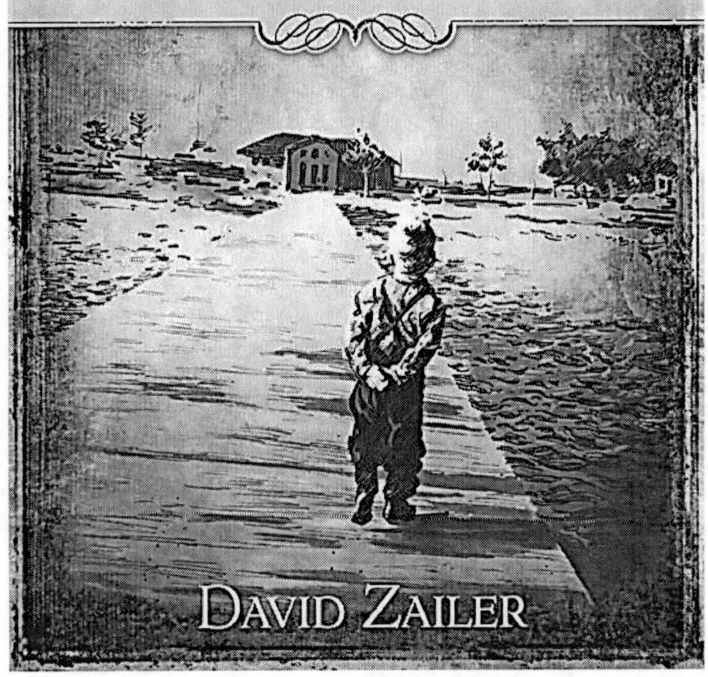
David Zailer

CPSIA information can be obtained at www.ICGtesting.com
Printed in the USA
LVOW082108180613

339165LV00004B/482/P